RADICALLY REVISED
VERSION
2.0
ENTIRELY ENHANCED

THE HAPPY HUSTLE™

1😵 ALIGNMENTS

TO AVOID BURNOUT & ACHIEVE BLISSFUL BALANCE

Cary Jack

SB PRESS

Published by Storybuilders Press

Revised Edition
Paperback: 978-1-954521-51-3
EPUB: 978-1-954521-52-0

*Dedicated truly to you. I pray this
helps you systematically harmonize your
ambition & well-being so you can put
the Happy in your everyday Hustle!*

SCAN ME

Check out **thehappyhustle.com/hub** for additional
regularly updated resources, and claim over $350
worth of bonuses included with this book to help
you operationalize your insights.

WHAT DOES HAPPY HUSTLIN' MEAN TO YOU?

"Happy Hustlin' to me means loving the life you have
while you create the life of your dreams."

Hal Elrod

USA Today *International Bestselling Author,
Keynote Speaker, and Podcaster*

"Working towards being able to do
what I want, when I want, with who I
want—that is Happy Hustlin'."

Pat Flynn

Wall Street Journal *Bestselling Author, YouTuber with over
100M+ views, and Award-Winning Podcaster*

"Happy Hustlin' means living the life that
you love, waking up every day and working
hard but enjoying the journey."

Candy Valentino

Wall Street Journal *Bestselling Author, Real Estate
Investor, and Serial Entrepreneur*

"Win then play. Act as though you have already won.
That is the game, and that is Happy Hustlin'."

Garrett Gunderson

Multiple time New York Times & Wall Street Journal
Bestselling Author, Wealth Strategist and Comedian

"Creating from a place of purity that supports
your life, that is The Happy Hustle™."

Dan Martell

Award-winning SaaS Entrepreneur, Angel Investor, and Bestselling Author

"Happy Hustlin' is when you have fulfillment in doing what you love."

Kiana Danial

CEO of Invest Diva & Wall Street Journal Bestselling Author

"Trust God. Enjoy your blessings at the end of the day,
and appreciate the ride; that is The Happy Hustle™."

Ben Greenfield

*World-renowned Health Expert, International Speaker, and
New York Times Bestselling Author of 13+ books*

"Getting to do the work you love, with the people you
love, when you want to do it. Knowing happiness is
available to you at any moment, and it's our choice
to really claim it; that is Happy Hustlin'."

Amberly Lago

*Viral TEDx Speaker, Bestselling Author, and Leading
Expert on Resilience and Transformation*

"Happy Hustlin' means that I am anxiously engaged in good work.
I'm not lazy; I'm not content; I'm making this world a better place,
and I'm hustlin' to do it for both my happiness and others."

Randy Garn

New York Times Bestselling Author, Serial Entrepreneur, and Angel Investor

Going after what you want, the way you want to do it, and knowing it's a privilege in life. That is Happy Hustlin' to me."

Alex Banayan

#1 International Bestselling Author & Youngest Business Author in American History

"Happy Hustlin' means you're working hard, having fun, and making an impact while being filled with joy and excitement along the journey."

Tia Graham

Keynote Speaker, Bestselling Author, and Founder of Arrive At Happy

"Working hard with freaking purpose is so beautiful, you know. I love working hard, and I love working hard in alignment with my purpose. It just feels like fuel; it's one of my sources of life, so working hard with a purpose is what Happy Hustlin' is all about."

JP Sears

Award Winning YouTuber, Comedian, Author, Speaker, Podcaster, and World's Most Lovable Ginger

"Happy Hustlin' means that you must work like it depends on you and you pray like it depends on God. I believe God has a plan for your life. But guess what? Your hard work and hustle are part of that plan."

Jon Gordon

15x Bestselling Author, Global Keynote Speaker, Leadership Expert

TABLE OF CONTENTS

INTRODUCTION

Ultimate freedom. Financial abundance. Loving relationships. Everyday fulfillment. That is what this book is all about. Unfortunately, though, the lion's share of people are not experiencing those things. Most people are just living for the weekend. Watching the clock tick. And working just for the paycheck. According to research, 3 out of every 4 employees feel disengaged and unhappy with their work.[1] And 80% of entrepreneurs feel like they work too much and are on the brink of burnout.[2]

See, there is a global epidemic of soul sacrificing taking place currently. The majority of people don't find their work as meaningful as they desire and feel they are settling. And news flash—most of us will spend over 81,000 hours of our lives working! The only thing we invest more time in is sleep.

So whether you're an employee or an entrepreneur, we all spend A LOT of time working. But that doesn't guarantee "eudaimonia" as the ancient Greek philosopher Aristotle calls it, modernly translated as human flourishing or a combination of well-being, fulfillment, and happiness, is going to be a part of the picture.

That is why this book was created: to simply help you put the HAPPY in your HUSTLE in a tested and proven way. **By definition, The Happy Hustle™ is systematically harmonizing ambition & well-being.**

Let's quickly define terms so we're all on the same page, pun intended. Systematic means the execution of a fixed plan or system methodically. Harmonization means the pleasing arrangement of parts in congruence. So, to achieve the harmonization of life's many parts, you need a methodical plan. Fear not; it's in the pages to come, and it isn't just a feel-good theory; it's a tangible road map.

Now, ambition is that strong desire to achieve something great, requiring determination and hard work. That's the hustle part. Well-being, on the other hand, is the state of being comfortable, healthy, and happy.

Combine all that together, and you've got the systematic harmonization of ambition and well-being. And that's the essence of The Happy Hustle™.

You might ask, *How do we make this systematic harmonization of ambition and well-being happen?* It's all in The S.O.U.L.M.A.P.P.I.N.™ System revealed in the following chapters. This proprietary framework is designed to help you balance the 10 key areas of life, while also revealing how you can transcend in each. That means blissfully balancing life, both personally and professionally, and enriching your reality in the process. So welcome to The Happy Hustle™, my friend!

First things first, I want to establish that this isn't your average step-by-step, "I will show you how to..." blah blah, BS self-help book. So toss those expectations out the window right now.

Real talk: This book was written not only to tell you, but to actually teach you. To not just be words on a page, but to cut through life's noise and speak to your soul. To provide you with a road map, a system, a way to Happy Hustle a blissfully balanced life, both personally and professionally—a life full of passion, purpose, and positive impact. This book includes Alignment Takeaways, Happy Hustle Hacks, Daily Actions Tasks, and Powerful Resources (plus a ton more) you can immediately implement to enrich your reality.

YOU SEE, BALANCE EQUALS HAPPINESS, AMIGO.

I didn't spend 2 ½ years writing this (plus another year revising, updating, and adding science & stats in this Version 2.0) for kicks and grins. I want it to mean something to you. I want it to help you, your family, your friends, and your team become true Happy Hustlers. You will legitimately be able to pick it up, flip it open to any page, and get real value. You will be able to go back and reread it when you drift off, find yourself out of alignment, or need a reminder.

I fully realize you are busy, and, if you're like most people, have roughly an 8-second attention span. Heck, you've probably already thought about 3 other things, and we're only on the introduction. Because of that, I've intentionally added attention-grabbing quotes, memorable acronyms, cheesy comedic one-liners, and lots of pictures to keep you on track so you actually finish this book.

You see, **balance equals happiness**, amigo. I know balance gets a bad rap, but I really do believe this to be true, and when you're done reading this book, I think you will too. And I promise you, if you stay with me to the end, you can achieve blissful balance both personally and professionally and avoid burnout. Yes, this book will solve the age-old, infamous, work/life balance problem while helping to change your life in the best way.

Well, technically, this book itself isn't going to do diddly-squat for your life. Absorbing the content and *implementing* The S.O.U.L.M.A.P.P.I.N.™ System (don't worry, we'll get into it) is what's gonna do it for you. But YOU gotta take action. YOU gotta take accountability for your reality. Are you game?

If you're not, stop reading. Real Happy Hustlers are always honest. So if you're out, meaning you want to continue with the potentially imbalanced and unfulfilling reality you've created for yourself, that's cool—I've still got love for you and wish you nothing but the best. However, if you are *in* and ready to commit to finishing this book and taking massive action throughout the process, *then let's freaking go!*

THE PROBLEM

Chances are you're not exactly where you want to be. You may feel like your work/life balance is completely out of whack. Or worse, you may feel like you're hustlin', but definitely not happy. That's actually the case for a huge majority of people in the global workplace, and it shows up as what the Gallup organization calls "disengagement."

UP TO 79% OF EMPLOYEES (THAT'S 3 OUT OF EVERY 4!) FEEL DISENGAGED WITH THEIR WORK. THAT'S INSANE!

In their recent *State of the Global Workplace* report[1], Gallup shared the following mind-blowing statistics: Up to **79%** of employees (that's 3 out of every 4!) feel disengaged with their work. That's insane! Employees who are not engaged cost the world an estimated **$7.8 trillion** in lost productivity. (That's trillion. With a T. Let that sink in.) Stress and overwhelm are at an all-time high, with **44%** of employees globally reporting *significant* daily stress. Not to mention, a recent study by Silver Lining found 75% of entrepreneurs and small business owners are concerned about their mental health.[3]

Any of those statistics resonate? Are you feeling disengaged and stressed from your work? Maybe a bit imbalanced in your life? Notice the importance of this book and putting the Happy in your Hustle? See if any of the following sounds like your current reality:

- You want more fulfillment and meaning in your life, but you don't make time to volunteer for causes you believe in or to selflessly serve others.

- You don't have the physical, emotional, and/or mental well-being you know is possible, but you don't exercise regularly or implement healthy habits consistently.

- You spend too much time with your television, laptop, or phone, scrolling social media or watching pointless TV shows or movies, rather than living in the present moment.

- You don't have the loving, pleasure-filled personal relationship you desire, and your family/friend connections are lacking or "complicated."

- You know you should meditate or have a mindfulness practice of some sort, but you fail to do so consistently and think you just don't have time for daily inner work.

- You sometimes financially struggle to make ends meet, let alone pay off the student loan/credit card bills/debt you have accrued. Or if you do have some money in the bank, you don't have a system in place to assure financial abundance.

- You know you should be investing in your personal growth, but you often waste your free time instead of using it to learn new skills and absorb valuable content.

- You want to have more fun and enjoy hobbies regularly, like martial arts, fishing, dance lessons, or oil painting, but you feel guilty whenever you do anything for yourself.

- You feel uninspired with your work, hustlin' but not happy. You work long hours and feel out of balance because you prioritize "success" over faith, family, friends, fitness, and fun.

- You spend the majority of your time indoors, under man-made toxic blue lights, breathing recycled air, getting beamed by electromagnetic fields (EMFs), or commuting in your vehicle, but not nearly enough time in nature connecting to Mother Earth.

Whew, that was a lot, I know. Any of those bullet points hit home? Good. I wanted to lay it all out here early and be real with you. Now *you* have to be real with *me* by being real with *yourself*. (Say whatttt?)

Which of the above is the biggest pain point in your current reality? Make a mental note, because each bulleted topic above represents an area in your life that may be misaligned. Don't worry, though—in the pages to follow, I'll show you how to get back in alignment with all 10 so you can Happy Hustle in all areas of life. Once you've put that blissfully balanced oxygen mask on yourself, you'll be ready to assist those around you (your family, friends, team, etc.) to do the same! But it starts with you.

Now you may be saying to yourself, *Cary, who the heck are you to show me the blissfully balanced promised land?*

Well, I may not have all the answers, but I do have some. People often ask me how I escaped the 9-5 daily grind to live a purposeful and prosperous life on my terms. Or how I get paid to do the things I love to do—all while juggling three successful businesses that have generated millions of dollars, hosting a top 0.5% globally ranked podcast based on downloads (*The Happy Hustle™ Podcast*), being a professional model/actor, and consistently creating inspirational and educational content designed to positively impact the world.

I also volunteer regularly, travel often, and enjoy hobbies routinely—like fly-fishing, soccer, and martial arts—the whole time attempting to show up as truly the best husband, father, brother, son, dog dad, and business leader that I can be.

I've worn many titles, but non greater than being a father to Kaizen and a husband to Steph

I can do all of this because I leverage a proven system, purposefully prioritize, and put the Happy in my Hustle. I place FREEDOM & FUN at the forefront of my decisions. And I focus on systematically harmonizing my ambition & well-being.

You can, too. Wherever you are, and wherever you're going, The Happy Hustle™ is the way. The Happy Hustle™ is how you overcome the stress, anxiety, and overwhelm from trying to do it all without a strategy. It's the way to systematically create your dream reality while avoiding burnout along the journey. It's how to have a life of balance, freedom, financial abundance, and fun! I know, I know, it seems too good to be true. But keep reading, and you'll see how The Happy Hustle™ worked not only for me but for thousands of others around the world!

HAPPY WORKERS ARE AT MINIMUM 13% MORE PRODUCTIVE, AND COMPANIES WITH HAPPY EMPLOYEES OUTPERFORM THE COMPETITION BY AT LEAST 20%.

And again, it's not just about you, personally. If you're leading a team of people, you should know that a study recently published in the *Journal of Happiness Studies* shows employee well-being and happiness accurately predicts employee performance. Happy workers are at minimum 13% more productive. Companies with happy employees outperform the competition by at least 20%.[4] So not only is Happy Hustlin' good for you, but it's good for business! Are you starting to recognize the importance of you and your team Happy Hustlin'?

Now, let me be straight up, as I will be throughout this book: I am still on my journey, Happy Hustlin' towards my glorious grand vision. I'm constantly in search of self-development and growth. Nonetheless, *I am happy*. I am happy within the hustle, and I live an amazingly blessed life.

However, it wasn't always this way for me...

See, before I was Happy Hustlin', I was just hustlin'. As a former NYC tech entrepreneur who fell victim to the ever-growing entrepreneurial burnout, I was once working 100+ hour weeks, getting roughly 5 hours of sleep each night, and grindin' my face off for profit, ego, status, and success—all the things society deems to be important.

However, it wasn't until I actually landed the 7-figure VC funding deal and partnerships with Microsoft and IBM for our innovative tech startup that I realized I was extremely unhappy and unfulfilled. After many tears and a gut-wrenching conversation with my business partner, best friend, and brother, Grant, I made a massive pivot.

We said no to the funding, folded the company, and I moved to Bangkok, Thailand for 10 months. It was there that I figured out a better way to work and live in alignment. A way to have my cake and eat it, too. A way to find happiness within the everyday hustle while doing something meaningful. That is where Happy Hustle was born.

So I'm speaking from experience here, as someone who literally burned out from NOT Happy Hustlin'. **That's why I felt called to write this book. I wanted to demonstrate the replicable journey anyone struggling with imbalance and unhappiness can emulate to transform their reality into a blissfully balanced life they love.**

Within these pages, I share my proprietary framework, which I call The S.O.U.L.M.A.P.P.I.N.™ System. I created this first for myself in order to Happy Hustle a blissfully balanced life after burning out. Then I began sharing it with others who witnessed my transformation and wanted it for themselves.

Fast forward to now, where The S.O.U.L.M.A.P.P.I.N.™ System is being implemented by countless people around the world, from corporate CEOs and their teams who want to increase employee engagement, happiness, and productivity through better balance, to entrepreneurs on the brink of burnout, and every working professional in between.

The different elements that make up The S.O.U.L.M.A.P.P.I.N.™ System will be revealed and explored in the pages to come, but let me at least get you started with *The 10 Alignments,* the foundation of S.O.U.L.M.A.P.P.I.N.™ Remember those bullet points from a few pages ago, and how some of them might have hit a little too close to home? Well, each one is based on one of The 10 Alignments and paints a mini-picture of what misalignment could look like.

THE S.O.U.L.M.A.P.P.I.N.™ SYSTEM IS BEING IMPLEMENTED BY COUNTLESS PEOPLE AROUND THE WORLD, AND IT CAN WORK FOR YOU, TOO!

S.O.U.L.M.A.P.P.I.N.™

The 10 Alignments of a Happy Hustler make up the acronym S.O.U.L.M.A.P.P.I.N.™—your soul's map to the blissfully balanced promised land!

SELFLESS SERVICE

OPTIMIZED HEALTH

UNPLUG DIGITALLY

LOVING RELATIONSHIPS

MINDFUL SPIRITUALITY

ABUNDANCE FINANCIALLY

PERSONAL DEVELOPMENT

PASSIONATE HOBBIES

IMPACTFUL WORK

NATURE CONNECTION

Now, you may have read the list of Alignments and thought to yourself, "I am definitely missing a few of these in my life." Well, don't worry. You can actually identify which elements you may be lacking at **thehappyhustle.com/hub.**

This quick assessment will show you exactly where your life is out of balance in real time. It's time to Happy Hustle in alignment with your true self's desires, while simultaneously serving a cause or causes that speak to your soul. You can live a blissfully balanced life of passion, purpose, and positive impact, and we're going to get into how, but first...let me properly introduce myself.

JACK OF MANY TRADES

I feel it's only right to give you a little backstory on who the heck I am. I've been a hustler since a very early age. My siblings and I were taught that if you want something, you have to earn it.

I am the product of two entrepreneurial parents: my mother, a chiropractor who owned a thriving practice, and my father, a mechanic by trade who owned a busy repair shop and automotive parts business. I learned first-hand what it takes to run your own business and the work ethic necessary to succeed by often working in the businesses. Both worked hard and earned modest middle-class incomes, which allowed us to have our basic needs met.

My father was strict. He was an old-school man of discipline. The second oldest of 6 kids, he left home when he was 16. He grew up hardened by his circumstances. He carved his own path and intended for us to do the same.

My mom lost her mother to cancer at an early age. Her father was busy running a fine menswear store and was a part of the Freemason society. Consequently, he wasn't around much throughout her childhood. She had to hustle to make it on her own, as did my father.

I grew up splitting time surfing & skating in the beach town of Sarasota, Florida with my mom and hunting, fishing, camping, and cowboying in the mountains of Red Lodge, Montana on my father's ranch. This is where I first learned the art of a balanced lifestyle.

I didn't have the easiest of childhoods (but it could have been a lot worse), as my early years were filled with a disastrous divorce, chronic family mental illness, scarring emotional and physical abuse, and moving 24 times before the age of 18. I was dropped on my head as a baby (probably explains a lot), which prevented me from stringing words together and caused a severe stutter. I would get so frustrated due to my inability to speak that I developed anger issues, OCD, and had to go through years of therapy and counseling. Nonetheless, I did have love and support from both parents, and I am very grateful for the adversity, as it made me into the man I am today. My entrepreneurial mentality was forged by my environment, and it naturally translated to hungry ambition.

I share this list of random income-earning activities I have done to showcase my journey, as it doesn't matter where you start, but where and how you finish:

- **Lawn Mower:** My first real dollars earned were in exchange for cutting the neighbors' lawns. Oh, the sweet smell of fresh-cut grass still brings me back...

- **Lemonade Stander:** Slangin' juice to the locals and passersby in the neighborhood.

- **Construction Worker:** Digging ditches, sweeping floors, and swinging hammers resulted in one calloused hand.

- **Smoothie Barista (at Smoothie King):** Consistency is key with any great smoothie. *Side note: I was hired and fired in the same week at this first W2 paying "real job" because I often liked to do things my own way. And I dropped the tub of bananas. This set me up to aspire to be my own boss.*

- **Soccer Trainer/Camp Counselor:** Being a pretty decent player myself, I started first working as a trainer to the youngsters, then went on to create my own soccer camp business in my early teens. I loved teaching the youth, especially playing "hitters and dodgers," where you line the kids up and beam balls at them while they attempt to dodge, occasionally pegging one or two of them off their feet! (Don't worry—they loved it, and no one sustained any permanent injuries.)

Coach Cary in action

- **Ice Cream Scooper (Coldstone Creamery):** Where I would sing for tips and wore my first (and not last) banana suit.

- **Sanitarian Technician (aka dishwasher):** Talk about pruney fingers.

- **Expo Chef:** Making house salads like nobody's business.

- **Bus Boy:** Where I mastered the art of carrying multiple plates at one time.

- **Restaurant Server:** Learning customers' non-verbal communication and understanding body language is essential for top tips. Plus, I believe being a waiter is good life training and everyone should be required to do it so you learn how to respectfully interact with staff.

- **Flair Bartender:** Dancing on top of the bar was the norm; it's also when and where I realized the entertainment value of shaking drinks in silly ways and how it boosted tips exponentially.

Getting flown down to bartend at the Corona Sunsets party on the beach in the Dominican Republic didn't suck.

- **Smoothie Barista (Round 2 - Jamba Juice):** Wheatgrass and oatmeal were perks of the job. This is where I wore my second banana suit—legit a full-body banana suit with face and armholes.

- **Distributor:** Mainly for goods that were previously illegal; it taught me the value of supply and demand economics. Won't get into this one too much. ;)

- **Italian Restaurant Server/Bartender:** Specialty cocktails began to be a thing around this time, so I started learning mixology.

- **WGN News Network:** News anchor internship in college (not paid, but gained experience).

- **Comcast SportsNet:** TV sportscaster internship in college (also not paid, but gained experience).

- **Nightlife Party Host/Promoter:** One of the best jobs I ever had. Literally, I got paid to party.

- **Male Dancer:** Yes, use your imagination. Think of a less-choreographed version of Magic Mike. ;)

- **Catering Worker:** Serving and bartending for catered upscale events, where I made a ton of contacts with the 1% and would often eat the untouched leftovers off people's plates. Hey, I was hungry!

- **Brand Ambassador:** Representing and promoting some of the largest brands in the world at pop-up events (Hermes, Burberry, Topman, D-Squared, Ted Baker).

- **Promo-Model:** More casual gigs, smiling and being personable in clothes of all sorts, usually for larger-scale events at stores like Neiman Marcus, Saks Fifth Avenue, Nordstrom, etc.

- **Professional Model:** Formal bookings; I got paid to have my image taken, usually for magazine, internet, or video publications (Lifetime Fitness, City Furniture, Cadillac, too many to list). At one point, I was represented by some of the top talent agencies in the world, Wilhelmina and Next Models.

- **Professional Commercial Actor:** Formal commercial bookings, where I would often play characters while promoting various nationwide brands (Corona, Home Depot, Jeep, Allegra, Tire Kingdom, Michelob Ultra, etc. You can see my professional reel at caryjack.com/actin).

Clean shaven Cary doesn't come out too often anymore, but here's a headshot from when he did.

- **Soccer Coach:** Actually got certified to officially coach. My #1 goal: keep every kid alive! But in all seriousness, I always enjoyed teaching the beautiful game to young players.

- **International Tour Guide:** This was actually a dream job. My brother and I spent 100+ hours learning Portuguese, building our resumes, and creating a video, all to land a job in Rio De Janeiro, Brazil for the 2014 World Cup. Four months of paid pure pleasure followed.

Grant and I had some of the best times of our life in Rio de Janeiro, Brazil while working a dream job during the 2014 World Cup.

- **Startup Entrepreneur:** This was my title for roughly 8 years as I started and stopped 4 legit companies. I love business and using it as a force for good, but it took me a while to figure it out, failing forward throughout.

- **Website Developer:** I managed and built a couple of websites in my day for some quick cash. I am now grateful for the experience, as I have leaned on it while delegating the building of my own business websites and helping advise others with their online presence.

- **Online Entrepreneur:** The digital age is upon us, friends! I have created and sold courses, e-books, audio products, podcasts, digital products, masterminds, and more on a variety of topics from modeling, to self-improvement, to sales, to fitness, and lots of randomness in between. I love being location independent and being able to work from anywhere with a Wi-Fi connection.

- **COO & Health Coach for a Leading Biohacking Company:** Diving deep down the rabbit hole of human optimization, I've helped clients from Olympic Gold Medal Athletes, to Fortune 500 CEOs, to soccer moms all over the world optimize their mind, body, and spirit using a mixture of ancient wisdom and modern science. This was a nice mid-7-figure business with a top-rated podcast; 65K copies of my business partner's book sold through a Free + Shipping book funnel, and millions of social media views and followers, which provided tons of insights and ultimately a proven path for The Happy Hustle™ to follow in the future.

One of the gigs I enjoyed greatly was working as a Biohacking Health Coach for amazing entrepreneurs and athletes. But it was especially rad working with these badass hockey players, Jonathan Toews and Duncan Keith, both multiple-time Olympic gold medalists and Stanley Cup winners. They are the best of the best at what they do as well as super cool and kind dudes.

- **Online Salesman**: I sold more than 3 million dollars of products and services (some mine, some affiliates) over 1-to-1 Zoom calls from 2018 - 2021, working typically less than 20 hours a week, and I've continued growing sales volume year after year ever since. Sales are the lifeblood of any business, and I happen to love the art of the deal. Want to make more money? Get good at sales. More on this later.

- **Co-Founder of Ecobreakthroughs:** I have created multiple businesses with my brother and currently am fighting the plastic pollution epidemic and climate change while using our business (ecobreakthroughs.com) as a force for good.

- **Marketing Copywriter:** One of the more valuable skills any entrepreneur could learn and implement. Even with ChatGPT and AI, a human copywriting touch goes a long way. Using words to inspire action in all of your content is non-negotiable in business. I've done this for myself and other companies.

- **Podcast Host:** Host of the 5-star-rated, top 0.5% globally ranked podcast, *The Happy Hustle™ Podcast*, where I interview high-performing entrepreneurs, spiritual gurus, and world-class Happy Hustlers who  are living a life of passion, purpose, and positive impact while manifesting their dreams—and share how you can, too! If you haven't already, I strongly suggest checking it out, available on all podcast platforms. #shamelessplug

- **Author:** Hence, this book, which has been a real labor of love, let me tell ya.

- **Personal Brand & Sales Strategist:** I worked with an awesome company called Brand Builders Group, which helps individuals turn their reputation into revenue. I started as a client, building my own personal brand under their guidance, and now have helped others using their transformative system to launch, grow, and monetize. Side note: Strategically aligned partnerships are one of the fastest ways to expedite your success and increase your income.

⦁ **Happy Hustler:** A lifestyle entrepreneur living a blissfully balanced life of passion, purpose, and positive impact while helping others do the same! My mission is to implement The S.O.U.L.M.A.P.P.I.N.™ System into the lives of 10 million+ Happy Hustlers worldwide to help them systematically harmonize ambition & well-being!

I know, quite the list...lots of lessons learned! And for the record, I fully realize I have been blessed from birth, compared to much of the world, by just being born a white male in the USA, which I do not take for granted whatsoever; yet, it was still a humbling journey to get here!

DON'T LET YOUR CURRENT WORK DICTATE YOUR JOY.

I share that laundry list of past gigs to show you that it doesn't matter where you've been or where you are; it matters where you're headed and what you are willing to do to get there. As long as you keep going and improving every day, work is work. We all gotta eat and keep the lights on. It's a part of life, and especially as a Happy Hustler, you do whatever it takes. As the old saying goes, if you can't get a seat at the table, serve water instead! I have "served plenty of water." It's all a part of the process.

That said, whatever it is you do, don't let your current work dictate your joy. If you're not happy with what you're doing, that's ok. Sometimes we all have to do things we don't necessarily want to. Sometimes that means wearing a banana suit, shoveling gravel, answering phones, going door-to-door selling things, serving food/ drinks—fill in the blank.

The act of hustlin' to make money and pursue financial freedom (aka life on your terms) will keep you humble and hungry; I know it has done so for me. Here's a quote by yours truly that sums up my mentality:

YOU HAVE TO EARN THE RIGHT TO DO WHAT YOU LOVE.

I found out early in my life that I didn't fit neatly into an employment box. Somehow, in most of my jobs, I would tend to discover what I deemed a better, more efficient way of doing the task at hand. I would end up doing it my way. That didn't always sit well with my employers who didn't really value the innovation.

So, I decided to work more freelance gigs, odd jobs, and just hustle to make my own path. This isn't the path for everyone, but for me, working odd jobs meant I could decide when and how I worked. It's definitely not the most secure way of living, because you never really know where your next paycheck is coming from—but no one said being an entrepreneur came with job security.

All of the random jobs I listed are just a part of my journey. From free food at catering jobs, to free products from promo-modeling, to free experiences by being a brand ambassador, to free lessons from business colleagues, I would soak up whatever I could from every opportunity.

Not to mention, I rubbed elbows with the "elite" and expanded my network all the while; I always engaged in conversations regardless of my uniform. Whether I was wearing an apron or a suit, I made sure to remain confident and unapologetically myself. Know that each job comes with some form of payment besides the monetary component, so take stock of what you're doing right now for money and discover value in other mediums.

I look for the positive with each hustlin' endeavor both past and present. I do my best to make as many connections throughout the process, many of which have translated to lifelong, mutually beneficial connections.

Opportunities come from all angles. Whether bartending or digging ditches, I am grateful for this roller-coaster of a ride. Earning my way, Happy Hustlin', staying humble and hungry.

Don't get me wrong, though—you don't have to be an entrepreneur, a CEO, or an independent contractor to Happy Hustle! Earlier I shared the statistic stating three-fourths of all employees feel disengaged from their work. Even if that is you right now, it doesn't have to be!

When you understand the principles of Happy Hustlin', and apply them to wherever you are and whatever you're doing to earn a living, you're naturally going to increase your happiness. And if your colleagues or team members are Happy Hustlin' too, even better! As they say, a rising tide lifts all ships. Happiness is truly contagious. I've seen it in action, my friend, and I can tell you—the benefits of a team full of people Happy Hustlin' are *exponential*!

HAPPY HUSTLER ASSESSMENT: SET THE FOUNDATION FOR YOUR HAPPY HUSTLIN' JOURNEY.

Now before we go any further, I've gotta ask: *Have you taken the assessment yet?*

If you breezed over the initial Happy Hustler Assessment call to action (thehappyhustle.com/hub), here it is again—only you can't escape it, since I put it in the book! Muahahaha.

Let's identify where you are in your life and where you may be lacking, so we can prioritize change accordingly, shall we? This will be your baseline and is an absolutely pivotal piece to the puzzle. I want you to get real, tangible value right from the get-go with this book. That means you're going to have to do some self-quantification.

Let's start by measuring where you rank in each of The 10 Alignments of a Happy Hustler. Be honest with yourself here. **Remember, what you measure you can manage.**

As you go through the following questions, score yourself on a scale of 1-5 in each of The 10 Alignments using this rubric:

10 ALIGNMENTS SCORE RUBRIC:

5 = A *Crushing It & Happy Hustlin'!*
4 = B *Satisfied & Making Progress*
3 = C *Ok & Getting By*
2 = D *Slackin' & Need to Step It Up*
1 = F *Significantly Lacking & Must Prioritize Change in This Area*

For each of the following questions, score where you rank in this area 1-5, and write it in your journal or on your note-taking device. Think about each in terms of the past 30-days timeframe.

1. ***Do you practice Selfless Service?*** Do you help causes and people who need it? Do you volunteer and donate to others who are less fortunate? Or have you been living more for yourself and not making time to give?

2. ***Do you have Optimized Health?*** Do you have the body, mind, and energy you desire? Do you exercise and eat healthy daily? Or have you been slacking?

3. ***Do you Unplug Digitally?*** Do you regularly do digital detoxes, putting your phone on airplane mode, closing the laptop, turning off the TV, removing the headphones and just being fully present? Do you set limits on screen time and create device-free barriers when you wake up in the morning and before you go to bed? Or maybe you know you have a tech addiction and are constantly connected?

4. *Do you have Loving Relationships with your significant other, family, and friends?* Is there plentiful pleasure and love with your partner? Do you regularly spend quality time with your kids, family members, and friends, being fully present with them? Or are you distracted, multi-tasking, and thinking about other things while spending time with those you care most about?

5. *Do you practice Mindful Spirituality?* Do you feel connected to a higher power? Do you meditate, practice mindfulness, and have an attitude of gratitude? Or do you feel disconnected and lacking faith in something bigger than yourself?

6. *Do you feel you are Abundant Financially?* Do you spend, save, and invest wisely? Do you have the financial ability to do what you want, when you want, with whom you want? Or do you feel financial stress and a lack of resources to live your dream reality?

7. *Do you focus on Personal Development?* Do you consistently read, listen, and watch educational and inspirational content? Do you acquire new skills and knowledge to better yourself? Do you spend time with inspiring people who raise your vibration? Or do you feel you are digressing or stagnating in your development?

8. *Do you have Passionate Hobbies you do regularly?* Do you have fun and routinely take part in activities you enjoy? Do you fill your cup with things that bring you joy that are non-work related? Or do you feel guilty spending time and money on hobbies for yourself?

9. *Do you currently have Impactful Work?* Do you have a career that fills you with joy and fulfillment? Do you feel you are working in alignment with your higher calling? Or do you feel disengaged and unhappy with the work you currently do?

10. *Do you have a Nature Connection?* Do you frequently get outside and tap into your true primal self? Are you a conscious consumer, voting with your dollar, purchasing products/services from sustainable companies? (Yes, that's part of it!) Or do you spend the majority of your time indoors, unconsciously consuming and feeling detached from nature?

See, that wasn't so bad! You should have 10 scores. Now, tally up your total score by adding each of the 10 scores together. If you are a 39 or below, sorry, but you are not yet a Happy Hustler. That means you ranked yourself BELOW a 4 or a 5 in most of The 10 Alignments. Give yourself grace as this is your new baseline. This should also be quite telling, revealing what area(s) of life you are lacking the most in. Allow this not to discourage you but rather motivate you to prioritize positive change accordingly!

Now, if you scored 40 or above, then congratulations! This means you are currently a Happy Hustler! Yahoo! That means you ranked yourself ABOVE a 4 or a 5 in most of The 10 Alignments. But let's not get complacent. Everyone can improve. Read this book in its entirety and determine what you can do to increase your score even more!

BLISSFUL BALANCE BOTH PERSONALLY AND PROFESSIONALLY IS NOT A FINITE DESTINATION BUT A NEVER-ENDING JOURNEY.

After taking your initial assessment, I recommend re-assessing once a week. I like to measure myself on Sunday evenings. I'll think back over the past week and then prioritize change accordingly for the week ahead. I suggest you do the same, as blissful balance both personally and professionally is not a finite destination but a never-ending journey. We are constantly evolving and need frequent, consistent, weekly measurements in each Alignment in order to accurately assess and then course-correct on our Happy Hustle voyage.

I know it seems repetitive, but do you know what else is repetitive and very necessary? Showering and wiping your butt. Treat this similarly.

Again, if you would like to take the most updated version of the Happy Hustler Assessment online and get your scores sent directly to you, go to **thehappyhustle.com/hub**. Then rinse and repeat every week (at minimum every 30 days) to keep tabs on how you're progressing.

 PRO TIP: I set a calendar reminder for every Sunday evening to remind myself to take the Happy Hustler Assessment and save the link as a favorite on my browser so I can access it easily. This ensures I accurately track my scores in each of The 10 Alignments in real time and make changes if needed.

Now, let's really get into the juicy goodness of The Happy Hustle™. I'm talking about each of The 10 Alignments in depth. So despite what you scored, you can really take control of your life and maximize every day with The S.O.U.L.M.A.P.P.I.N.™ System. We're kicking things off with Selfless Service, one of my personal favorites, so buckle up y'all,—*it's go time!*

HAPPY HUSTLE BLISSFUL BALANCER

I know you are hungry for more in your life. I know you are a learner and someone who wants to become a better version of yourself, or else you wouldn't be reading this.

If you want help Happy Hustlin' and keeping yourself accountable to a blissfully balanced life, then I HIGHLY recommend not just taking the Assessment once a week, but also picking up one of our Happy Hustle Blissful Balancer fridge magnets. This whiteboard fridge magnet is a constant reminder of the Daily Action Tasks you need to complete in each of The 10 Alignments in order to blissfully balance your day, thus your week, and thus your life.

This isn't a ploy to get you to purchase more stuff from me. This was specifically created to complement the book and actually help you implement The S.O.U.L.M.A.P.P.I.N.™ System into your daily life. I made it analog by design, meaning it's not an app or tech tool, and that was specifically to

help get you off your devices and back to the present moment. (Plus, I'm assuming you open your fridge at least 3x a day, so this will be a constant reminder.) It really can make a positive difference when utilized consistently. Get a Blissful Balancer for yourself, your family, friends, and team at **thehappyhustle.com/hub** or scan this QR code:

SCAN ME

And if you're ballin' on a budget currently, you can just print out a new PDF each week from thehappyhustle.com/hub (although eventually, that would be a waste of paper) and tape it on your fridge for FREE.

Remember, what you measure you can manage. Measure your balance, because again, **balance equals happiness,** my friend. You're probably going to get sick of me saying that, but I bet you'll remember it by the end of the book.

HERE'S AN EXAMPLE OF A FILLED BLISSFUL BALANCER.

HAPPY HUSTLE™
BLISSFUL BALANCER
BALANCE = HAPPINESS

S.O.U.L.M.A.P.P.I.N™ CHALLENGE

WEEK OF: September 20th-26th

PERSONAL GOAL OF THE WEEK: Do at least one random act of kindess everyday.

PROFESSIONAL GOAL OF THE WEEK: Make over 10k in net revenue!

THIS WEEK'S MESSAGE TO MYSELF: Be present and grateful every moment, you never know when it could be your last.

10 ALIGNMENTS	ACTION TASK	M	T	W	T	F	S	S	SCORE
SELFLESS SERVICE	Give 15 minutes of time/expertise to someone in need	X	X	X		X		X	5
OPTIMIZED HEALTH	Exercise for 25 minutes and drink 1 gallon of water	X		X	X	X	X		5
UNPLUG DIGITALLY	Don't touch devices for the first 30 mins after waking up		X	X	X			X	4
LOVING RELATIONSHIPS	Send a gratitude text to one person you care about	X	X	X		X	X	X	6
MINDFUL SPIRITUALITY	Meditate for 10 minutes, focusing on your breath and gratitude		X		X		X		3
ABUNDANCE FINANCIALLY	Send email to one new perspective client/partnership opportunity	X	X	X	X	X	X	X	7!
PERSONAL DEVELOPMENT	Read inspirational and educational book for 20 minutes	X	X	X	X	X		X	6
PASSIONATE HOBBIES	Participate in 1 fun activity that brings you joy		X	X	X		X	X	5
IMPACTFUL WORK	Post 1 inspiring social media content sharing your message	X	X	X		X	X		5
NATURE CONNECTION	Go for a walk outside without your device for 15 minutes	X	X	X	X		X	X	6

Add up daily X's for total weekly Alignment score. Prioritize change accordingly. Score rubric: 7=Ultimate Happy Hustler, 6=Happy Hustler, 5=A, 4=B, 3=C, 2=D, 1=F

"HAPPY HUSTLE YOUR DREAM REALITY AND LIVE A LIFE OF PASSION, PURPOSE, & POSITIVE IMPACT!"
WWW.THEHAPPYHUSTLE.COM

HAPPY · HUSTLE

CHAPTER ONE

ALIGNMENT 1: SELFLESS SERVICE

The secret to living is giving.

Tony Robbins

I want to tell you a story. Not to impress you, but to impress upon you the significance of giving. In 2016, my brother, Grant, went to rural Guatemala and visited a small Mayan village on beautiful

Lake Atitlan where our mom was living (she's an old hippie at heart and loves to travel). Like my mom, Grant instantly fell in love with the people and culture.

Many of the indigenous locals there live on less than $1 a day, have very little access to education or opportunity, and 7 out of 10 children suffer the effects of chronic malnutrition. Grant came across a local non-profit community center that provides lunch every weekday to the most at-risk individuals to strengthen and stabilize the weakest members of this impoverished community.

After speaking with the founders and directors, he learned that they were in desperate need of help. My brother agreed to join the team as a business consultant, bringing along my sister, Megan, as a non-profit consultant, my wife, Steph, as a brand and communications specialist, and me, to help with the marketing and implementation to revamp the organization and further its impact.

Grant put his MBA skills to the test and did a deep audit of the business. He collected and analyzed all the data points of their organization, which were basically hand-written notes in three different languages (Spanish, English, and Katchiquel—their local dialect) without any clear organization, filing, or accounting systems.

He quickly realized how in shambles they were. After crunching the numbers, Grant identified over $52,000 dollars in missing donation money! His instincts told him something was fishy about one of the American women executives in charge of the financials, but he never expected this.

It was sickening to think about how the children served by this organization live on less than a dollar a day, how far that missing money could go, and how this greedy woman was laundering the donations into a private account to apparently buy local property. Following some serious detective work, and with extreme tact, Megan and Grant approached the non-profit board members and the organization's director with proof of the missing money and who had taken it. They were all shocked.

They prepared to file a lawsuit against the woman, ordering the money to be returned. She knew she was caught, and so did her lawyer father. To avoid the charges brought forward, her father covered her by rightfully returning every penny. She was promptly ousted from the organization.

After the smoke cleared, it was time for us to get busy and rebuild the non-profit. Steph, Megan, Grant, my mom, and I all donated time, money, and expertise to help the cause. We organized a massive online fundraiser, hosted a local community event, redesigned the organization's website and logo, created captivating content, participated in new and improved programs with the kids, and so much more.

This experience had a profound impact on my life. I can still recall the pure joy of being in Guatemala, giving to those deeply in need. The smiles on those kids' faces still bring me joy today. As Tony Robbins says, "Success without fulfillment is the ultimate failure." And one of the fastest paths to fulfillment is to help others.

SERVICE-OVER-SELF MINDSET

Living a life of passion, purpose, and a positive impact is what The Happy Hustle™ is all about. The positive impact you have on others and the world is ultimately what creates true happiness and a feeling of fulfillment. The peace & happiness you seek in your heart is found in knowing you lived for more than just your personal aspirations. So, depending on where you ranked yourself in the Selfless Service Alignment (remember 1-5?), tune in closely, because this one is a genuine game-changer.

> **LIVING A LIFE OF PASSION, PURPOSE, AND A POSITIVE IMPACT IS WHAT THE HAPPY HUSTLE™ IS ALL ABOUT.**

The service-over-self mindset is one of the most powerful gifts I could ever hope to help awaken within you. That's why I am a proud Rotary Club member, one of the largest volunteer organizations in the world. Their motto is indeed just that: "service above self." I recommend researching & joining a club in your area.

If you read this book and are left with nothing else but a determination to adopt this mindset, I would consider the 3+ years spent writing this bad boy completely worth every minute. The ripple effect of spreading your joy touches far beyond those you immediately serve.

With enough people getting on board the service-over-self express train to transcendence, we can balance and harmonize the world while raising the collective vibration. Love is the way, and service is the GPS. Let service guide you to a higher purpose, and an empathetic, enlightened existence. If you're currently feeling stressed, or caught up in your schedule and workload, consider selflessly serving others, and chances are you'll feel instant relief.

FULFILLMENT COMES WITH SERVICE

You may be thinking, "But Cary, I can barely cover my bills every month, let alone give anything to others." Trust me, I get it. But as they say, if you won't give 10 cents out of a dollar, you probably won't give $100 out of a thousand, or 1 million out of 100 million. Service is like a muscle; it needs to be trained to grow. I've done plenty I'm not proud of in my life, but one thing I have done that I am proud of is adopting the service-over-self mindset long before I had money to give, so I know it's possible.

GIVE

INSIGHT

FINANCES

TIME

GIFT—GIVE INSIGHT, FINANCES, & TIME

Give Insight

Let's say money is tight currently...no worries. Sharing your insights and expertise has the potential to be the most rewarding of all. By giving your insight, you can change the trajectory of one's life indefinitely. You have acquired knowledge, skills, and abilities that are unique. Sharing these with others can be powerful, not only for those with whom you share, but for you as well.

There's an old proverb that states, "Give a man a fish, you feed him for a day. Teach a man to fish, and you feed him for a lifetime." Who can you teach to fish? Whatever "fishing" is for you, mentor those in need, and bless your life with fulfillment.

Steph (my wife) and me supporting our troops by giving insight and sharing The Happy Hustle™ message to a group of soldiers while on a US Military base in South Carolina

Give Finances

If you have your basic needs met, a roof over your head, food in the fridge, and clothes on your back, chances are you can allocate funds to give *something* to others in need. I know, you're thinking, "But Cary, when I have a million dollars, I will *for sure* give to others in need; it's just that right now, money is a little sparse."

Truth Bomb: The more you give, the more you'll get. It's real, my friend. I know it seems counterintuitive, but I have seen it time and time again in my own life and in others' lives. Giving is good karma. The time is *now*. Don't wait to give. Live in abundance, and know that the universe will always manifest more. Find a cause that you can donate to today, and give 10% of your last paycheck. You'll witness the full-circle effect. Trust me.

After playing soccer with these awesome kids in one of the poorest slums in Cartagena, Columbia, Steph and I donated time and money to help further their education.

Give Time

Arguably the most valuable commodity you could ever give is your time. You cannot replenish time like you can money; therefore, the value is incomparable. If you have more time than money right now, donate your time.

Sign up to be a mentor for a child in need, feed the homeless, work at an animal rescue, or do anything else that speaks to your heart and soul. Try out several, and then decide where you wish to serve. At the time of this writing, I give my time volunteering to help kids with exceptionalities (Down syndrome, autism, etc.) with an Adaptive Horsemanship Program. I basically teach these amazing humans to ride horses, but oftentimes they teach me more about life. The act combines two things I love—horses and helping. Plus, the heart-warming feeling I receive when I see the smile on the kids' faces is truly priceless. It's worth mentioning that giving your time may not always be "easy" or "fun," as you may experience difficult or challenging elements in the service of your cause. But it *will* be fulfilling, so persevere anyway.

SCHEDULE GIVING

The best way to ensure you give regularly is to schedule it. You can schedule weekly visits (giving time) or regular mentorship phone or video calls (giving time and insight). You can set up recurring payments (giving finances) from your bank account to non-profits of your choice. I've found that creating calendar reminders that prompt me to donate my insights, finances, and time is extremely effective.

 PRO TIP: One creative way to schedule your financial giving is through KIVA. You can provide donations directly to social and environmental entrepreneurs in developing countries and impoverished areas. The best part is that 100% of your money goes directly to the person you are supporting, and it's all automated, so it withdraws from your account each month. I've personally been donating through KIVA for years via recurring monthly withdrawals. KIVA also allows you to make a loan to an individual in one of these areas, and when that loan is paid back, you can repurpose it to help another individual. So cool!

ACCOUNTABILITY THROUGH COMMUNITY

Another way to ensure you are actively practicing the service-over-self mindset is by creating accountability through the community organizations or people you serve. Let's say you join the Big Brothers Big Sisters organization, and you forget to pick up your little brother or sister on your scheduled day. Knowing you let them down, you're most likely gonna feel terrible and surely not want to disappoint them in the future. Or if you have a group of people you volunteer with who are depending on you to help, that extra accountability and social component can positively ensure you do what you say you're going to do. Just like with your work, if you want to put the Happy in your Selfless Service Hustle, you need to take accountability & be disciplined.

ONE OF THE FASTEST PATHS TO FULFILLMENT IS TO HELP OTHERS.

⊛ ALIGNMENT TAKEAWAY

One of the fastest paths to fulfillment is to help others. Think **GIFT: G**ive your **I**nsight, **F**inances, and **T**ime, and witness your happiness skyrocket!

APPLY THE 5 STEPS TO HAPPY HUSTLIN' IN EACH ALIGNMENT

Remember earlier how I mentioned that what you measure you can manage? So, here's where the rubber meets the road. It's time to learn how to measure your success in each of The 10 Alignments, starting with this one, Selfless Service.

And here's how we're gonna do it—with *The 5 Steps to Happy Hustlin'*. You can leverage the 5 Steps to increase your score/success in each of The 10 Alignments to move you from wherever you are to where you want to be.

- **Step 1:** Do an honest audit of your reality, where you are right now when it comes to the Alignment. Give yourself grace if needed, but recognize the change that is possible.

  Example: "I haven't really volunteered in years. I have been spending most of my money on my family and myself. I have been just so busy with work that, unfortunately, I haven't created any time to give. I ranked myself a 1 (the lowest score) in the Selfless Service Alignment."

- **Step 2:** Define your vision for success in the Alignment. What does a 5 (a top-ranking score) actually look like for you here? Be definitive by setting a SMART goal: **S**pecific, **M**easurable, **A**ttainable, **R**ealistic, and **T**imely.

  Example: "I want to make Selfless Service a priority. My goal is to volunteer my time a minimum of once a week for an hour to a cause I care about, and give 10% of my paycheck each month to a foundation I believe in. I also want to create my own non-profit by the end of this year."

- **Step 3:** Reverse engineer the process to achieve your SMART goal, and create a strategy of small, sequential momentum-building steps you can take toward creating a 5 reality in the Alignment.

Example: "For me to achieve my goal in this Alignment, I need to: 1) Research the causes I want to give my time and money to. 2) Schedule the time on my calendar and show up at the given time to volunteer. 3) Set up a recurring payment each month giving to the foundation I chose. 4) Create a non-profit business plan. 5) Name the organization. 6) Research & adhere to the legal steps to creating a non-profit. 7) Serve our cause with the non-profit!"

- **Step 4:** Take action and execute! Manage your time & priorities accordingly.

     Example: Follow the strategy steps created!

- **Step 5:** Employ persistent consistency. Enjoy the journey Happy Hustlin' a blissfully balanced life of passion, purpose, and positive impact.

     Example: Commit to small consistent daily progress! "I will serve others with my time, finances, and new non-profit organization!"

Now, obviously, the examples above are abbreviated. I urge you to go into as much detail as you want, but not more than you need. Don't get bogged down in the game plan so much that you get analysis paralysis. Just get er' done.

So let's go ahead and jump in with Alignment 1: Selfless Service. Start a notebook or journal and start working through the steps. Aside from following the 5 Steps to Happy Hustlin' to create a 5 A+ reality, I'm going to share some Daily Action Tasks to Happy Hustle in each Alignment to help get your juices flowing. Think of the 5 Stages of Happy Hustlin' as the main course and these Daily Action Tasks as the appetizers to a deliciously balanced meal!

THE 5 STEPS TO HAPPY HUSTLIN'

HAPPY · HUSTLE

1
DO AN HONEST AUDIT OF YOUR REALITY. FIND GRATITUDE FOR WHERE YOU ARE.

2
DEFINE YOUR VISION FOR SUCCESS; WHAT DOES A 5 LOOK LIKE IN THIS ALIGNMENT?

3
REVERSE ENGINEER THE PROCESS AND CREATE A WINNING GAME PLAN.

4
TAKE MASSIVE ACTION AND EXECUTE! MANAGE YOUR TIME AND PRIORITIES ACCORDINGLY.

5
PERSISTENT CONSISTENCY. ENJOY THE JOURNEY HAPPY HUSTLIN' A LIFE OF PASSION, PURPOSE, & POSITIVE IMPACT!

☑ DAILY ACTION TASKS TO HAPPY HUSTLE:

Selfless Service

1. Spend 15 minutes giving your time or sharing your expertise with someone who could benefit from it.

2. Smile and give a genuine compliment to a stranger.

3. Drop a Random Act of Kindness by *anonymously* buying something small or doing something kind for someone else.

😃 EMBARRASSING FUN FACT

I have been court-mandated to volunteer 2 times in my life. Once for being a bad boy (not going to get into it, but I know I learned the hard way), and once for speeding on my motorcycle after getting pulled over going 178 mph, which resulted in a *very* large fine, a 3-cop pullover, and 100 community service hours. Now, instead, I volunteer by choice!

The selfie smirk of someone who has 3 state troopers behind him after being pulled over going 178 mph on his motorcycle… lesson learned.

🧠 POWERFUL RESOURCES

Books:
Building Social Business by Muhammad Yunus
Give Work: Reversing Poverty One Job at a Time by Leila Janah

Podcast:
Giving Back Podcast

Movie:
Schindler's List

HAPPY HUSTLER SPOTLIGHT 🔦

- Leila Janah -

Born to Indian immigrant parents, the inspiring social entrepreneur, Leila Janah was driven by the belief that "Talent is equally distributed, but opportunity is not." She is a shining example of Selfless Service in action.

She founded Samasource in Kenya, with the mission to improve the lives of those living below the poverty line. The company has helped more than 50,000 people lift themselves out of poverty and has become one of the largest employers in East Africa.

Besides Samasource, Janah was the founder and CEO of LXMI, a fair-trade, organic skincare company, and Samaschool, a non-profit organization that trains people in digital skills. Leila spearheaded a global impact sourcing movement and was a champion for environmental sustainability and ending global poverty.

Leila Janah, inspirational social entrepreneur

She also wrote a powerful book called *Give Work: Reversing Poverty One Job at a Time*, which is well worth the read!

Beautiful both inside and out, sadly at the young age of 37, due to complications from epithelioid sarcoma, a rare soft-tissue cancer, Janah died on January 24, 2020. Her commitment to creating a better world was unparalleled. She was indeed a Happy Hustler, and the ripple effects of her Selfless Service will be felt for generations to come.

CHAPTER TWO

ALIGNMENT 2: OPTIMIZED HEALTH

Take care of your body; it's the only place you have to live.

Jim Rohn

Optimizing your health is essential for success in every area of your life. When you are sick, almost everything else takes a back seat. That's why focusing proactively on embodying a healthy lifestyle is imperative to Happy Hustlin' your dream reality.

I learned the principles of a healthy life at an early age as a competitive athlete. My whole life was focused on high performance. I knew that if I wanted to excel on the field, I must prioritize my health and wellness off the field. If I didn't sleep well, I knew my performance the next day would be negatively affected. If I didn't eat right and stuffed my face with junk food, the next day I would be sluggish and off. If I didn't work out consistently and skipped days, I knew my energy would be different, and come game time, I would be functioning less than optimally. I'm sure you can relate to how much better you feel and perform when you exercise regularly and eat clean.

> **I KNEW THAT IF I WANTED TO EXCEL ON THE FIELD, I MUST PRIORITIZE MY HEALTH AND WELLNESS OFF THE FIELD.**

Soccer is and has been my passion. It was my dream to play professionally. I even went as far as training to play in the Olympic Development Program as a US National Team hopeful. I started playing at the age of 3 and instantly gravitated to the sport's non-stop action and intensity.

I was never the best player on the field, but I always strived to be the hardest working. At an early age, older teams would recruit me to play with them. We won many championships, and I was usually asked to be the team captain.

I was playing for a high-level club travel team in which we competed in all the state and national competitions. I was positioning myself for an NCAA Division 1 scholarship, and my goal was to get a full ride. I spent hours a day practicing, watching films, and submitting to scouts. When it came to my senior year of high school, expectations were indeed high, especially since our team won the state conference title the year prior and became the team to beat, returning the majority of our starting players.

It was our first home game of my senior season. I was the captain of the team, starting center-midfielder, and ready to give my all. With college scouts in the stands and an NCAA Division 1 scholarship at stake, it was GO time. The whistle blew. It wasn't more than 15 minutes into my first game as a senior when it happened. I was attempting to block a clearance from one of their defenders with my left foot. As I lunged to block the ball, the defender kicked the ball and followed through into my foot, sharply inverting my unplanted ankle. I (and the players around me) heard an ear-piercing pop. I screamed in pain and instantly dropped to the ground, holding my ankle.

I tried to get back up but couldn't. My teammates helped me over to the sidelines, and I knew it was bad. My ankle immediately swelled up to the size of a grapefruit, and I couldn't put any weight on it.

My season was over. My previous Division 1 college scholarship offers were swept out from under me. The reality began to sink in at the doctor's office where the X-rays revealed I had broken my ankle. Later, an MRI revealed that I also had torn two major ligaments. My dream of becoming a professional was over.

After much rehab, I was still able to solidify a college scholarship and enjoyed 3 years as an NCAA collegiate player. In my 4th year, I moved to Barcelona to study abroad and continue playing overseas. In my broken Spanish, I convinced the head coach of a local semi-pro team to let me try out and proceeded to have one of the best performances of my life.

I ended up making the team, playing around Barca for a bit, and getting paid a small salary per game. I wouldn't say by any means that I fulfilled my dream of playing pro, but I did get paid to play, and that was cool.

Although my ankle injury plagued my career, I'm very grateful for that time in my life. I still have to wear braces and wrap my ankles every time I play, but at least I can compete on Sundays in Men's League (where I still GO HARD!). The point here is that life doesn't always turn out how you intend. **Plans change. Things happen. But without Optimized Health, you won't be able to perform at your peak.**

EXERCISE

NUTRITION

ENVIRONMENT

REST

GALLON

YOUTH

I thought I was destined for soccer greatness. I thought I was physically and mentally able, but one injury can change it all. Regardless if I'm playing professional sports or not, I know that my health is essential to my happiness and to creating my dream reality. And it is for you, too.

E.N.E.R.G.Y.

Regardless of how you measured yourself on the Assessment for the Optimized Health Alignment, we can all agree on the importance of consistently improving your health. Happy Hustlin' your health is all about E.N.E.R.G.Y., which taken as an acronym could just be the catalyst for you to reach a whole new level! The acronym calls out 6 critical components of Optimized Health: Exercise, Nutrition, Environment, Rest, Gallon, and Youth.

Exercise

Look, this isn't technically a health book so I'm not going to overcomplicate it. Whether you want to do CrossFit, hot yoga, HIIT workouts, strength training, running, swimming—you name it—the most important aspect of exercise is just doing something to move your body consistently, at least 25-45 minutes every single day.

Your goal should be to sweat and increase your strength, flexibility, and functional movement. Elevate your heart rate in each of your workouts to the point where you need to breathe out of your mouth, not just your nose. Doing this trains your body to move oxygen and blood to your muscles more efficiently and effectively.

Breathing and diversification are key to my uber-simple exercise training philosophy. I make sure to switch it up and confuse my muscles with various exercises to avoid plateaus and stagnation while maintaining my size and strength. You can often find me doing bodyweight exercises like handstands, planks, push-ups, and pull-ups, as those are the cornerstones of my routine. I then like to layer in kettlebell work, steel mace flow, TRX bands, punching and kicking (both on a heavy bag and shadow boxing), and groundwork (like bear crawls and animal movements) to keep it interesting.

The key to it all is consistency. Move your body every day.

 PRO TIP: If you spend more time watching other people sweat (ie: sports on TV) than sweating yourself, it's probably a good indicator that you need to level up your exercise frequency and get your ass in the game.

Nutrition

You've heard the saying: You are what you eat. Well, it's freaking true in many regards. I cannot stress enough the importance of eating healthy, organic fruits, vegetables, and whole foods.

If you could only do one thing right now to optimize your health for the rest of your life, I would say making the shift to a whole food, natural diet would have the greatest impact.

Yes, that means cutting out the processed crap. No more sodas, sugar candies, junk food, etc. If you can't pronounce every ingredient on the label, you probably shouldn't eat it! Now, you're probably saying, "Geez, Cary, no Oreos or Coca-Cola is a real buzz kill! That sounds extreme!"

Listen, I'm all for sweets, and I'm not saying you can't have them every once in a while, but just choose to make them natural sweets. You can use naturally sweet apples to make an organic apple cobbler. You can make coconut milk ice cream with natural cacao nibs. You can eat papaya and watermelon with nothing but a spoon.

The point is, if you want to be a Happy Hustler, you have to find ways to be conscientious about what you put into your body. Every single bite has an effect, either positive or negative, whether you notice it or not. I recommend not getting caught up with the latest fad diet, but rather, focusing that attention on simply eating, juicing, and blending an all-whole food organic diet. Eliminate pesticides & GMOs by buying organic as much as possible. Then indulge in the occasional natural sweets. My guilty pleasure is fruit-filled muffins of all types. As Hippocrates said, "Let food be thy medicine and let medicine be thy food." Be diligent with your diet.

BE DILIGENT WITH YOUR DIET.

Environment

Sadly, most people don't realize that it doesn't matter how much you exercise or how strict you are with your healthy diet; if your environment is full of toxins, your health will suffer. The big environmental toxins to look out for are mold, chemicals, EMFs, water, and air quality. If your home or office or wherever you spend the most time are riddled with any or all of these, then you will not be able to optimize your health.

Mold is often caused by water damage. It is present in most homes and needs to be remediated. Chemicals are present in most beauty & household products, which disrupt the endocrine system when used. EMFs are emitted by our devices (cell phones, laptops, TVs, etc.) and break down our cellular DNA which causes an array of issues such as headaches, loss of concentration, sleep disturbances, and more. And water & air quality issues can drastically affect our performance, especially if your water has chemicals, or inorganic material that basically slowly poisons you with every sip and breath.

Not trying to be the bearer of bad news here; it's just the hard truth. Most of our environments have some or all of these toxins. So what can we do about it? Well, optimize your environment. **I recommend checking out testmyhome.com to learn how you can better protect yourself and your family.** Then consider ordering their Home Test Kit (which tests for mold, chemicals, EMFs, water & air quality, and more).

You can use the discount code HAPPY to save some $$. I did a podcast episode with the founder, Ryan Blaser, on *The Happy Hustle* episode #291 to go deeper on the topic. Regardless of whether you use this company or another, just do yourself a favor and test your environment. Then, based on the findings, prioritize the necessary steps to optimize it!

Rest

Poor sleep affects performance in a multitude of ways. When you are sleep deprived, you may experience a decline in mood, difficulty concentrating, and impaired memory. Deprive yourself of sleep over a long enough timeline, and you may witness poor work performance, cognitive decline, and even heighten your risk of dementia.

According to the American Academy of Sleep Medicine (AASM)[1], the amount of sleep you need changes based on your age, but adults 18 years of age and older need 7-9 hours of sleep each night for optimal health. No shocker here; however, the trick is actually getting it! So let's break down an uber-simple sleep routine I follow and recommend.

IF YOU WANT TO REALLY HAPPY HUSTLE A LIFE YOU LOVE AND HAVE THE ENERGY TO CRUSH YOUR GOALS EACH DAY, THEN PRIORITIZING YOUR SLEEP IS IMPERATIVE.

Start by tuning your circadian rhythm to get up and go to bed as close to the sunrise and sunset as possible. Then, when it is bedtime, turn off the tech (and yes that includes the TV) 30 minutes before bed. Use blue light blocking glasses to limit the blue light about 1 hour before bed, and stop eating or drinking about 90 minutes before bed. If you have trouble falling asleep, try reading a book, or, if you must, listen to a calming audio-only meditation. Just make sure you are sleeping enough, my friend. If you want to really Happy

Hustle a life you love and have the energy to crush your goals each day, then prioritizing your sleep is imperative.

Gallon

According to the National Library of Medicine, 75% of Americans are chronically dehydrated. Dehydration is a frequent cause of hospital admission and can cause morbidity and mortality on its own, not to mention it complicates many medical conditions.[2]

Water is essential for vital functions like bringing oxygen to your cells, regulating body temperature, and protecting vital organs and tissues. Plus, water is needed in the excretion of waste and basically every major bodily function. So that's why it's so important to drink enough quality water.

Most research suggests that just drinking enough water to quench your thirst may be sufficient; however, other studies recommend drinking a gallon of water each day as extremely beneficial for hyperhydration. Know that the amount of water needed varies per person, but in general, aim to drink between a half gallon and a gallon of water each day for optimal hydration.

Taking it a step further, the quality of water you drink matters. There are said to be 9 types of water: tap, mineral, spring/glacier, sparkling, distilled, purified, flavored or infused, alkaline, and well. Each comes with its own pros & cons, and without getting too deep in the weeds here about water, just do your best to eliminate toxins and make sure your water source is as clean as possible.

Youth

We live in an interesting time in history, where science and technology are advancing at an unprecedented rate. With that, the research on anti-aging and longevity has exponentially increased. I want to share with you some of the things you can do, that are rooted in science, to help you live a longer, healthier life.

According to Dr. David Sinclair[3], the co-director of Biology of Aging Research at Harvard Medical School and co-founder of several biotechnology companies, some core principles for aging and longevity include a healthy diet, exercise, meditation, cold therapy, and intermittent fasting. He even notes you can actually reverse aging by making healthy lifestyle changes in these areas.

Dr. Sinclair has a list of anti-aging supplements he recommends:[4]

- **Vitamin D3,** essential for many processes in the body, including bone health and immunity.

- **Omega-3 fatty acids,** important for heart health and cognitive function.

- **Resveratrol,** a polyphenolic compound that occurs naturally in the skin of red grapes, peanuts, and some other plants. It has been shown to have several health benefits, including anti-aging effects.

- **Probiotics,** bacteria that are good for your gut health. These "friendly bacteria" balance the presence of good and bad bacteria in a human microbiome shielding overall organismal health.

- **Nicotinamide mononucleotide (NMN),** a naturally occurring molecule needed to make NAD+. Besides obtaining it from food, Sinclair gets it from NMN supplements. He takes **1000 mg NMN daily,** which may be a high dose. Sinclair takes NMN with resveratrol and a spoonful of olive oil to make it more available.

- **Spermidine,** found in foods like cheese, legumes, mushrooms, and soy, impacts aging mechanisms. Spermidine is related to reduced risk of neurodegeneration, cardiovascular disorders, and cancer-induced death in humans.

- **Quercetin and fisetin** clear away what is known as senescent cells (cells that resist dying). These two strong flavanols serve as antioxidants and are known to reduce inflammation and tissue injury while aging.

- **Vitamin K2,** important for bone health and mitochondrial health. People can obtain this vitamin naturally from leafy greens, whole grains, and natural oils.

Disclaimer: Please do your own research on each and consult with a medical professional before taking anything. However, know that there is A LOT you can do proactively to combat aging and increase longevity on your Happy Hustlin' journey!

BIOHACKING 101

The term biohacking has become all the rage lately. To me, biohacking is a series of uncommon strategies to optimize your daily performance and fight fat, fatigue, and chronic illnesses. It's the act of utilizing ancient wisdom and modern science for total human optimization.

In reality, my mom was and is an OG biohacker. As mentioned, she is a chiropractor by trade but has earned a functional medicine degree as well as training from both Eastern and Western medical schools of thought. She raised us with healthy, organic foods and a holistic lifestyle. I distinctly remember always having herbal teas instead of sodas and vegetable snacks instead of junk food.

We rarely, if ever, took antibiotics, and she fought to avoid vaccinations. I have never been vaccinated, and I am still living, breathing, and thriving. We would heal ourselves naturally and use herbal and plant medicines to combat illness.

I have since studied holistic remedies, researched functional medicine, tested the latest alternative medicines, and little by little, ultimately biohacked myself to optimal wellness. Prior to starting The Happy Hustle™, I joined forces with a premier biohacking company as COO and have replicated the process of mixing ancient wisdom and modern science, helping thousands of clients all over the world regain and optimize their health using our proprietary system.

I BELIEVE IN THE HOLISTIC APPROACH TO HEALTH CARE WHENEVER POSSIBLE.

So, I am going to share with you some of my favorite biohacks for Happy Hustlin' your health based on the holistic biohacking mentality I have forged. For the record, unless it's an emergency, I do not take traditional medication, antibiotics, nor any other pharmaceutical drug. Even when I had my ACL, ankle, and 2 nose surgeries (I've had a deviated septum from breaking my nose fighting & surfing), I didn't even take the pain meds. I believe in the holistic approach to health care whenever possible.

My goal is to share with you what I do and hopefully provide a couple of actionable takeaways that you can apply to your life and health right away.

Naked Push & Pull

We're going to start simple. One of the things that I am religious about and have been doing for as long as I can remember is doing push-ups, pull-ups (if there's a pull-up bar nearby), and sit-ups before every shower. Yes, that means I usually end up doing them naked.

I do push-ups until it hurts—not necessarily to max out, but just enough to feel the burn, and then do 10 more. These bodyweight exercises are timeless, and you can do them virtually anywhere. Whether you are traveling and in a hotel room or staying at a friend's house, if there's a floor, you can do push-ups and sit-ups. So no excuses! Let's start a #nakedpushups movement, y'all!

Ice Baths

Two of my favorite ways to Happy Hustle my health are with cold and hot thermogenesis. That is a fancy way of saying ice baths and infrared saunas. The benefits of the ice baths are vast. Not only does hopping in a pool of ice-cold 40-degree water for 3 minutes mentally strengthen you, but it will increase the blood flow throughout your cardiovascular system. Also, ice baths decrease inflammation and burn calories as your body naturally will attempt to heat itself up.

I recommend, at the minimum, taking a cold shower once a day, or at least finishing each shower with 30 seconds of cold. In life, we have to do things we don't want to do. Each time I force myself to take an ice bath or cold shower, I am training my brain to do things I don't feel like doing but know that I need to, aka creating discipline and mental fortitude.

Remember: Discipline = Freedom, as Jocko Willink says.

Saunas

Infrared or dry saunas are an amazing way to detox your body and lose weight. Raising your core body temperature induces an artificial fever. How does this benefit the body? Well, fever is the body's natural mechanism to strengthen and accelerate the immune response. This enhances the immune system, and, when combined with the improved elimination of toxins and wastes via intense sweating, you'll increase your overall health and resistance to disease.

Soaking up some full-spectrum infrared red light in my Thera360 Plus Sauna

By sitting on your bum in a sauna, you are literally sweating out the toxins and increasing your metabolism in the process. Using a sauna can also decrease stress and increase muscle recovery. Increased blood circulation carries off metabolic waste products and delivers oxygen-rich blood to oxygen-depleted muscles, so they recover faster.

One of my favorite biohacks is my full-spectrum infrared sauna: Therasage Thera360 Plus.

You can get the hook-up when you use code HAPPY on everything at **therasage.com**. Plus, it's a family-owned company that actually cares about their customers!

Sunlight and Stretch

Every morning when you wake up, one of the best things you can do to kick-start your day is to get direct sunlight and stretch your body. Sunlight is the source of life's energy. When natural sunlight is absorbed through your skin, it triggers the body's production of Vitamin D, which is a crucial ingredient for your overall health. It helps protect against inflammation, lowers blood pressure, helps muscle recovery, and improves brain function—not to mention that it may even protect against cancer.

However, the key is not to get so much exposure that it results in sunburned skin, as that obviously has an adverse effect on your health. Natural sunlight can improve vision and repair your eyes. I sun gaze just about every morning for a couple of minutes in the downward dog position looking back and up through my legs about 45 degrees off the sun (not directly at it).

I then stretch—usually shirtless—in the sun. It is said that stretching every day can add years to your life. Stretching allows blood and nutrients to flow throughout your body, which reduces soreness and increases recovery. Stretching also helps prevent injuries and will improve your range of motion. So, get out there and touch your toes, baby! Even better if you stretch in the sun. It is a no-brainer to charge up your body in the morning.

If you're feeling especially froggy, throw some shadow boxing kicks and punches in there, do a little Tai Chi, or jam to your favorite tune and bust out an ecstatic dance. All these things will help your body and also elevate your mood. After all, we are Happy Hustlin' out here, so we might as well have some fun!

Supplementation

Most people are deficient in magnesium. Magnesium Breakthrough is my go-to.

Here's my take on supplements: less is more. If you can get the nutrients from whole foods, veggies, and fruits—do it. If you can't and need to supplement, be diligent with which supplements you use. Many supplements are crap and just an isolated form of the real deal. Read the labels and reviews before purchasing or consuming. Do your research and ask an expert if you're unsure about supplements.

It is also extremely beneficial to get annual blood tests. Some of the supplements that your ripped, healthy friend recommended may work great for them, but you have a completely different cellular DNA makeup, thus the importance of testing and not guessing. When you know your lab results, which include your vitamin and mineral deficiencies, the environmental and genetic mismatches, and the toxins that may be hindering your performance, then you can make educated decisions based on what you actually need.

Many people take too many supplements that often end up at best as expensive urine, or at worst, actually causing complications. Don't be that person! I take only the supplements I feel are necessary and that I cannot otherwise get from food, and when I do take them, they are scientifically validated, 3rd-party tested, and are based on my bloodwork needs. My point is, everything you put in your body has an effect. Be diligent.

There is one company whose supplements I use regularly, and that is BIOptimizers. They make a powerful probiotic called P3-OM, a digestive enzyme called MassZymes, and a properly formulated magnesium formula that is a game-changer for enhancing sleep, called Magnesium Breakthrough. These 3 are a staple in my routine. You can check them out at **bioptimizers. com/happy** to save you some moolah on these awesome products.

Final supplement note: if you want to get more done in less time, check out some brain-optimizing supplements. I use Nootopia brain-boosting pills for maximum focus, concentration, and creativity. They are 3rd-party tested, and they stand behind their products with a 365-day money-back guarantee. They have a bunch of unique formulations for different occasions. Check out Nootopia. com/happyhustle and get the hook-up. Again, I believe less is more when it comes to supplements, but there are definitely some I use to get & keep the Happy Hustlin' edge!

@ ALIGNMENT TAKEAWAY

You can have everything you want in this life and more, but in order to get it, you must have the **E.N.E.R.G.Y.** to work for it. Exercise, Nutrition, Environment, Rest, Gallon, Youth are the pillars for Optimized Health. Your energy is directly related to your cellular health, and your cellular health is directly related to your daily habits.

If you want to perform at the highest level in your particular field, then you have to exercise and eat healthy. Balance intense workouts with intense recovery. Do the little things, hold yourself accountable, and optimize that health, baby!

☑ DAILY ACTION TASKS TO HAPPY HUSTLE:

Optimized Health

1. Move your ass for a minimum of 30 minutes!

2. Intermittently fast: decrease your feeding window to 8 hours.

3. Stay hydrated: drink a gallon of purified water a day.

😆 EMBARRASSING FUN FACT

I once competed in a push-up contest on MTV's stage at Panama City Beach with a girl in a bikini sitting on my back. I know, douche alert. It was a different time back then, so cut me some slack… and for the record, I got second.

🧠 POWERFUL RESOURCES

Books:
How to Eat, Move and Be Healthy by Paul Chek
Own the Day, Own Your Life by Aubrey Marcus
Head Strong & *Game Changers* by Dave Asprey

Podcasts:
Ben Greenfield Life Podcast
The Model Health Show with Shawn Stevenson

Movies:
The Mind, Explained
What the Health
Food, Inc.
The Game Changers

HAPPY HUSTLER SPOTLIGHT 🔦

- Danette May -

I had the privilege of getting to know Danette May at a mastermind in Utah back in 2018. Her kind energy lit up the room, and we shared many of the same core values regarding health and nutrition, as well as our common upbringing in Montana.

She is not only a Happy Hustler, but is also America's leading healthy lifestyle expert, #1 best-selling author of *The Rise,* along with 7 health and fitness books and programs. And she is the co-founder and CCO of Mindful Health, LLC (#48 on the Inc. 5000 List), Earth Echo Foods, a dedicated founder of The Rise movement, a world-renowned motivational speaker, a wife, and a mother.

In addition to being named #16 on Women's Fitness list of fitness & health leaders for 2018, Danette was featured in the culture-shifting documentary, *WeRiseUP,* alongside His Holiness the Dalai Lama, Alanis Morissette, Marie Forleo, Richard Branson, and many other high-impact, accomplished leaders.

Since 2011, she's helped transform the physical, mental, emotional, and spiritual lives of millions of people around the world by focusing on healing foods, healing movement, and a healing mind. Her impactful mission is simple, yet profound! She and I both believe in the holistic approach to health and wellness. She inspires people to dig deep into their souls to find out who they really are, to construct the life of their dreams, and stand fully in their power. Danette and I would both agree, whatever you want in this life is all possible, but not without taking care of and optimizing your health!

CHAPTER THREE

ALIGNMENT 3: UNPLUG DIGITALLY

Disconnecting from our technology to reconnect with ourselves is absolutely essential for wisdom.

Arianna Huffington

O ne of the ways that I truly love to Happy Hustle is to go deep into the backcountry wilderness and completely disconnect from technology. My team and I host an event every year we call the *Montana Mastermind Epic Camping Adventure*. It's completely off the grid: no phones, no laptops, no service. We *disconnect* to *reconnect*.

The high-performing entrepreneurs who join us for this adventure hike more than 10 miles deep into the backcountry wilderness, typically climbing more than 3000+ feet in elevation gain. This is no walk in the park. Our cowboy friends pack in horses to carry in the food and group camping gear, and attendees carry in their own backpacks with somewhere between 30-50 lbs. in tow. We set up base camp around a pristine alpine lake in a stunning canyon, complete with 360-degree jaw-droppingly beautiful views. There we spend 5 days camping out while enjoying a structured yet flexible itinerary of mixing business with pleasure. We learn primitive survival training from an expert survivalist, such as bow-drill fire making, water purification, shelter building, hunting/gathering techniques, navigation, etc.

We practice the art of fly-fishing, as everyone who attends gets their own fly rod/reel combo. We do primal bodyweight workouts and natural cold plunges. We embark on powerful breathwork sessions and deep dive into enlightening mediations. We sprinkle in specific business masterminds throughout in order to workshop our adversities and share what's working in our businesses. Delicious and nutritious healthy food is catered throughout by a professional backcountry chef who makes a variety of wild game over a campfire. And we have an outdoor professional videographer and photographer to capture all the epic footage!

During this entire experience, we push ourselves both physically and mentally so growth is ever present. Yet members describe the experience as absolutely rejuvenating and a complete recalibration. Stepping outside of our comfort zones is how we evolve.

Most who've attended say it is "life-changing" and "an enlightening spiritual journey" and "invaluable to their overall well-being both personally and professionally." What they come to realize is that the sustained absence of being tethered to devices 24/7 makes all the difference. No texts. No calls. No buzzes or dings interrupt our focus or flow, just full presence in nature's glory.

It is said you are the sum of your closest relationships. Surround yourself with people who add value to your reality. Being around other rockstar entrepreneurs helps us mastermind our businesses and overcome personal adversity, which ultimately will expedite our success. Not to mention, when you surround yourself with like-minded inspiring souls in such an environment, lifelong bonds are forged. The truth is, it's a helluva great time mixin' business and pleasure while digitally detoxing deep in the backcountry wilderness. For those of you who are interested in joining in the future, you can go to **thehappyhustle.com/hub** and apply to see if it's a fit.

Regardless of whether you attend a Montana Mastermind Epic Camping Adventure or not, I recommend going off-grid for an extended period of time and tapping into your primal self and un-distracted soul. Unplugging digitally is absolutely imperative if you want to achieve a blissfully balanced life and be a true Happy Hustler.

The 2021 Montana Mastermind Epic Camping Adventure crew of rockstar Happy Hustlin' entrepreneurs!

PUT THE PHONE DOWN FOR A DIGITAL DETOX

One of the biggest things holding you back from viscerally connecting with yourself, others, and nature is that little rectangle made of plastic & glass in your pocket. Yes, I'm poorly describing your cell phone. That dang thing is what I like to call a time sucker.

It will suck all the time you give it and never give any of that time back. Your valuable minutes spent on the device could have been used elsewhere, like out in nature, connecting with people you care about, or in solitude. One of the best practices I've adopted each week is a digital detox on most Sundays. I refrain from using any phone, computer, tablet, TV, or any other device. I'll put all of them in a closet or drawer, completely out of sight, and not touch them until 24 hours have passed from the time that they went in. I make time to get outside and tap into my soulful self. I am still, present, and at peace. I highly recommend this for you, too.

We often don't realize just how inundated we are by the constant notifications, calls, emails, texts, alerts, news, social media dopamine dumps, and unconscious societal pressures that plague our every waking moment. It's like we are constantly plugged in. Even the strongest computers in the world need to power down and do a reset from time to time—and so do you!

When you do a digital detox, you will find the freedom and fulfillment that you so eagerly seek is already present within you. You don't have to go far. I find most high-performers are consistently lacking in this Alignment. So depending on where you ranked yourself in this Alignment, start to put the phone down more, get outside, connect with loved ones, and enjoy what really matters.

EMFS AND DOPAMINE

Since we're talking about unplugging digitally, we have to talk about the electric and magnetic fields (EMFs) our devices emit and the dopamine dumpin' that comes from using them. EMFs are all around us, and they affect our health. Our smartphones, computers, Wi-Fi routers, smart TVs, tablets, smartwatches, wireless headphones, microwaves, electric cars, etc., all emit EMFs. According to Science Direct[1], "repeated Wi-Fi studies show that Wi-Fi causes oxidative stress, sperm/testicular damage, neuropsychiatric effects including EEG changes, apoptosis, cellular DNA damage, endocrine changes, and calcium overload. Each of these effects are also caused by exposures to other microwave frequency EMF."

To mitigate your risk and exposure, you must be deliberate with how you use your devices. I recommend at the minimum unplugging your Wi-Fi at night, turning all of your devices on airplane mode when not using them, and spending time each day digitally detoxing.

 PRO TIP: You can buy a programmable wall timer that automatically will shut off your Wi-Fi router on a schedule. Just Google it and set it up. Super easy, and will help you Unplug Digitally.

It's also important to mention the effects of tech, and especially social media, on your brain. See, every time you get a notification, your brain sends a chemical messenger called dopamine along a reward pathway that makes you feel good. Dopamine is associated with activities like sex, food, exercise, love, gambling, and now, social media. The problem is that when your brain releases dopamine due to social media, it is weakening your brain's ability to concentrate and simultaneously causing you to become addicted to the "dopamine rush," which makes you want to check your phone constantly. The point is, resist the urge, and just unplug as much as possible. Use tech wisely, don't let it use you!

B.R.E.A.K.

Here's an easy acronym to help you remember how to Unplug Digitally: take a B.R.E.A.K.

BARRIERS

RECHARGE

ELIMINATE

AIRPLANE MODE

KEEP

Barriers

If you really want to become the master of your devices, then you must set barriers and actually stick to them! For example, a barrier for me is I do not touch my devices 30 minutes after waking up and 30 minutes before going to bed. This gives my mind, body, and soul time to be present without the distractions of technology during two of the most important parts of the day. Try doing this and watch your happiness increase. Even if you just start with 15 minutes in the morning and 15 minutes in the evening, you will notice a difference.

A key to adhering to the barriers you set for yourself is to have a consequence associated with it. According to The Pain-Pleasure Theory of Motivation[2], human nature seeks more to avoid pain than attract pleasure. **Consequences create commitment.** So when you have a consequence for yourself every time you don't do what you say you're going to do, you are more likely to commit the desired action.

For example, here are a couple of consequences I use for myself when I don't adhere to my barriers:

- Donate $1000 (or sometimes more) to the opposite political party or a cause I despise
- Eliminate my favorite foods from my diet for 1 month
- No TV, movies, YouTube, or social media for a week

Again, don't just set barriers; set barriers with consequences. This way you will do what you say you're going to and ensure you're Happy Hustlin' towards your dream reality!

Recharge

Just as your devices need to recharge, so do you! Make a point every day to create a minimum 30-minute recharging session. I like to leave my phone, computer, TV, headphones, and every other device behind and just go outside. If you can get sunshine during your recharge session, even better. If you want to Happy Hustle at your peak, you need to take breaks to recharge. I assure you the 30 minutes spent will actually improve your performance in your workday.

I also like to jump on my mini-trampoline for typically 5-10 minutes of my recharge session with inspirational music playing loudly. Now obviously, this works better if you have a home office, but who knows? Maybe your employer would allow you to bring a mini-trampoline into the break room. I recommend putting this recharge session on your calendar to ensure it gets done.

Eliminate

Entirely eliminating your devices from your day is difficult—I get it—but it is so, so necessary. I am not suggesting you just wake up tomorrow and don't use your devices, as I respect the fact that we all have work to do. With that being said, though, scheduling these elimination blocks ahead of time makes them more than possible.

> ## YOU'D BE SURPRISED WHAT YOU CAN ACCOMPLISH WHEN YOU ARE DISTRACTION-FREE.

For example, I like to schedule 7-day dopamine detoxes once a quarter, at minimum. For 7 days, I eliminate social media, TV, movies, podcasts, music, and really anything from a device that produces dopamine when consumed. I will plan content production and posting ahead with my team to make sure everything continues as it should. I will let my clients or business colleagues know I will be MIA. And I embark on the dopamine detox stress-free, knowing my business and work are good to go.

I gotta say, I typically make more money during these 7-day stints than the whole month combined. In one 7-day dopamine detox, I generated over 6 figures just because I was so focused and dialed in. You'd be surprised what you can accomplish when you are distraction-free. Give it a try for yourself and witness the benefits!

Airplane Mode

One of the best, most underutilized features on your phone is airplane mode. Just about every phone has this feature. This little feature can be a game-changer for your productivity. When you are not actively using your phone, I recommend turning on airplane mode, especially during focused work blocks where you need to be on it. This will block a cellular signal from coming into the phone. Plus, your phone will save battery life in airplane mode, so there's that. These little habits stacked can make a powerful difference in your performance, my friend.

Keep

Rounding out our B.R.E.A.K. acronym is the K: Keep your commitment to yourself to unplug digitally. This is where the big D word comes into play. Yeah, I'm talking about DISCIPLINE. It's great to create barriers for your device use, set up recurring recharge sessions in your calendar day, schedule elimination blocks such as a dopamine detox, and know about the airplane mode feature on your phone… but if you don't keep your commitments and stay disciplined, then all is for naught! So this one is the most important component of them all. As Tony Robbins says, "Knowledge is not power; knowledge is potential power. Knowledge is trumped every day by execution." So execute B.R.E.A.K. and keep your commitments to Unplug Digitally daily!

⊚ ALIGNMENT TAKEAWAY

Disconnect to reconnect. Being without phones, laptops, TVs or devices allows us to tap into our primal, present, true selves. I recommend doing regular digital detoxes from this moment forward and leveraging **B.R.E.A.K.** daily! Create Barriers, Regularly Recharge, Eliminate Excess, use Airplane Mode, and Keep Your Commitments to yourself.

DAILY ACTION TASKS TO HAPPY HUSTLE:

Unplug Digitally

1. Spend your first and last 30 minutes of each day device-free.

2. No phones at mealtime; enjoy your food and the company around you.

3. Keep your phone on airplane mode for a minimum of 1 hour a day during waking hours.

 # EMBARRASSING FUN FACT

I once lost my phone, wallet, and dignity while raging at a foam party in Ibiza, Spain. I didn't replace my phone for over a month, and that was one of the absolute freest times in my life.

 # POWERFUL RESOURCES

Book:
Disconnect to Reconnect: How to Unplug and Get Your Life Back by Carmine Migliaccio

Podcast:
The Happy Hustle™ Podcast—Episodes #78, #164, #166

Movie:
The Social Dilemma

HAPPY HUSTLER SPOTLIGHT

Cowboy Duncan Vezain

Now when it comes to being unplugged digitally, I gotta say it is hard to find a role model in this Alignment since it seems we are so plugged in all the time. But, if there was one for me, it would be my good buddy, one-eyed Cowboy Duncan. This guy is the toughest, most legit cowboy I know.

Cowboy Duncan Vezain, living life outdoors and working with horses and his hands

He lives his life outdoors, working with horses and his hands. He was born and raised in Montana and spends his time ranching, roping, riding bulls, competing in rodeos, building saddles, making leather goods, shoeing horses, building wagons, breaking horses, branding cattle, recording a music album, shooting movies, slangin' side-shooters, crackin' whips, you name it. Anything Western, this guy has done it! He works a lot with Hollywood movies and TV shows that are shot out West as the go-to horse wrangler and often as the talent, usually as the bad guy. (Due to his eye patch, it's a natural-looking role for him!) But that's not why I featured him in this Happy Hustler Spotlight.

He is unplugged digitally during the majority of his days. Despite being disconnected, he is reachable, and will always call you back, and do what he says he'll do. If he says he will be at the trailhead at 7:00 AM with five horses ready to ride, then by golly he'll be there. He has a website for his business. He has a phone number. And that's about it. No social media. No other BS. He makes handshake deals and is a man of his word. He's a family man with a beautiful wife and two amazingly independent daughters.

Steph and me swimming with Milo bareback in the "redneck water park," a muddy pond, on one of the annual Labor Day Wagon Trains in Montana

He lives a simple, hard-working, successful Happy Hustlin' life. He is an example of what is possible if you want to master a craft (or multiple) instead of playing the social media online guru game. He has positioned himself as THE guy for his skills in his area, and people reach out to him, as opposed to him marketing to them. I've seen first-hand this rewarding way of life, and I must say, oftentimes I am envious of the sheer simplicity. So, see if you can simplify your life by unplugging more from your devices, quieting all the noise that comes with them, and getting back to what's important.

Dunc and me on the annual Labor Day Montana Wagon Train, where we basically ride (and race) horses, drive wagons, and camp out for 5 days. Talk about some good ol' Western fun!

CHAPTER FOUR

ALIGNMENT 4: LOVING RELATIONSHIPS

We are most alive when we're in love.

John Updike

No matter how successful you become in your professional life, if your personal Loving Relationships aren't solid, you won't be Happy Hustlin' a blissfully balanced life. Hence, the importance of truthful, supportive, loving relationships on your Happy Hustlin' journey. I feel that I would be remiss if I did not share a love story in this book, so here we go.

Let me preface this experience by saying that I have had plenty of fun and have met a lot of women from all over the world. But never did I think I would fall so hard. It happens when you least expect it. It happens when you are at a place of true self-love. And it often happens when you aren't necessarily looking or ready for it.

For me, in particular, it started one warm sunny afternoon in South Florida, when I was booked for promo-modeling at The Breakers in Palm Beach. By "promo-modeling" I mean paid to walk around a room full of wealthy women with a pair of Manolo Blahniks (very high-end women's shoes) on a silver platter.

In the midst of my route, I locked eyes with a tall, brown-eyed beauty in a gorgeous glittery gown. I shamelessly approached her with my platter in hand and sparked up a conversation. Her name was Steph; she was from Uruguay, and she was a film actress. We hit it off—both being from Florida, both involved in the entertainment industry, both loving nature and the great outdoors, and both promo-modeling at the same event. We exchanged social media profiles, and that was that.

I continued my duties, as did she. The gig ended without much more than that initial exchange. Eight months went by, and I had moved to Bangkok, Thailand, where I was modeling and acting. One morning when I checked in on my socials, I saw that same little Latina heat, Steph, had commented on one of my modeling pictures. I had a pretty serious mustache and rattail at the time (as it is one of my favorite looks) while rocking a hipster, 3-piece suit getup. She commented, *Ok GQ, I see you over der. ;)*.

The comment that started it all

That was it. That was all I needed. I saw this comment from the other side of the world and couldn't get her out of my mind. I started lurking on her profile nightly (#creeper), and I said to myself, "I'm for sure hitting her up when I get back."

I returned from my Southeast Asian adventures and immediately began to plant the seed. I sent her a Facebook message just catching up with some small talk—a little back-and-forth banter, if you will. Since it had been a while, and I barely knew her, building trust was essential.

I then asked her to join me for a paddleboard and fishing evening excursion, followed by biking beach cruisers to Taco Tuesday...a pretty swell first date, if I say so myself. She initially responded enthusiastically, and the date was set.

But apparently, there was a miscommunication, which we still both laugh at and agree to disagree about what happened. Regardless, I proceeded to ready the paddleboards for this much-anticipated date.

5:00 PM (our pre-arranged meeting time) came and went. She no-called and no-showed me as I stood there waiting with my board shorts on and a fishing pole in hand. Yep, she completely stood me up.

After what felt like an eternity (truly only 1 full day) without a message explaining her actions, she finally texted. With seemingly little remorse, she said, "Sorry, got called into work." I replied with a firm message back stating how I value my time and how I would appreciate a simple message letting me know sooner next time so I don't wait around like a dufus.

As she now recalls, she was attracted to my confidence and the respect I insisted on, rather than putting her on a pedestal like many others had tried to do in the past. We then made plans for a rain check. I happened to be heading back home from a party at my cousin's house in Orlando and was passing by her home in West Palm Beach. We made plans for brunch because that was what timing allowed, and because who doesn't love a good brunch?

We hit it off right out of the gate. We learned more about each other as the conversation flowed effortlessly. When brunch wrapped, we shared a sweet kiss-less goodbye. I had a Home Depot commercial casting to attend, so I asked if she would want to meet up afterward for that elusive paddleboard fishing excursion. She was surprisingly free and up for the endeavor.

By the time we got to my house in Hollywood, Florida, it was too late for paddleboarding, so we opted for riding beach cruisers to Margaritaville (a restaurant on the beach). After making balloon hats with a girl on stilts (true story), we rode over to the Taco Beach Shack. We listened to live music, danced, and laughed.

As we biked home, it was bliss—nothing but good vibes. We hung out with each other practically all day—eight separate locations and activities. There was never a dull moment or a lapse in conversation. It just felt so right!

We both instantly knew something was different. It was a bit scary. Our theme throughout our initial couple of interactions and during the months to follow was, "Don't fight it." Naturally, our human nature says to protect yourself and keep your wall up to not let the other person know your true feelings. It's a game we all have played. But, when we adopted this "Don't fight it" concept, we just let ourselves and our emotions be free—no games.

We both fell hard. We even waited for intimacy, something I wasn't accustomed to doing. It just felt like we should wait until the perfect time. We didn't want to "ruin" it. We allowed our friendship to build and to really get to know each other, romancing each other's minds before the bodies. We connected on a deeply spiritual level.

My noble steed, Milo, and me, galloping up to the altar at my wedding with an American flag in hand screaming YEE YEEIII

And here's my beautiful wife and me sealing the deal with a passionate kiss in front of our closest family and friends for the ceremony inside the barn at our ranch in Montana.

Fast forward to 2021. Steph and I got married on our family ranch in Montana. I galloped up to the altar on my noble steed, Milo, holding an American Flag, screaming *yee yeeiii* while my beautiful bride stood elegantly in the barn, in front of 100 of our closest family and friends. Fast forward to now when we have a beautiful son named Kaizen and hopefully more to come. Being the best father and husband possible are my top Happy Hustlin' priorities. I knew that she was it from the very beginning. I was initially scared to let her know how I felt, but when you know, you know.

LOVE & 4 THINGS THAT DESTROY IT

What is all this Happy Hustlin' for if you don't have love in your life? Remember where you ranked yourself in Loving Relationships? Well regardless of if it was low or high, pay extra attention, as this Alignment is IMPERATIVE for happiness. See, the ironic truth of human existence is that no matter how much we accomplish or how much money we make, it is ultimately other people who give these accomplishments meaning.

IT'S THE LITTLE THINGS, DAY IN AND DAY OUT, THAT ADD UP OVER TIME TO UNSHAKEABLE FULFILLMENT OR UNSALVAGEABLE MISERY.

Every day your relationships are built up and torn down in the subtlest ways. It's the little things, day in and day out, that add up over time to unshakeable fulfillment or unsalvageable misery.

You decide how you treat the ones in your life that you care the most about. Do you take your significant other for granted? Do you put off calls with your family members? Do you spend half-assed, distracted time with your kids or best friends? Or do you do the opposite?

Realize that love needs energy to thrive. Sure, there will always be a special bond between a mother or father and their child. But this unconditional love, that most of us experience with our parents, often stops there. The other relationships in our lives, ones with partners, husbands, wives, boyfriends, girlfriends, siblings, and best friends, need our energy, time, and attention to act in a manner that fosters a loving connection. If you stop giving these relationships your energy, they will eventually stop providing you with deep love.

It's important to note that there are 4 main contributing factors that actually destroy loving relationships in your life. Think about which of the following are currently present for you and how you can pivot accordingly:

1. Lack of Trust

Do you do what you say you're going to do? Because every time you don't, it adds a crack to the windshield of trust until eventually, it will shatter completely. Trust is everything. Don't break it. Keep your word, whether that means doing the dishes as you said you would or showing up on time for your date. Once trust is gone, it's EXTREMELY difficult to get back.

2. Disrespect Towards One Another

Do you treat your loved ones as you would want to be treated? Don't say anything in the heat of the moment today that will hurt tomorrow. Since you know them better than most, you can cut them deeper with hurtful words. Be kind and respectful, even when shit hits the fan. I know that's easier said than done when we get overwhelmed. Often, the best thing to do when that happens is is to take time and space to cool off before conversing—more on this later.

3. **Criticism or Judgment**

Do you nitpick, criticize, and judge? Cut that crap out. Worry about yourself, not them. This is one I still work on. Don't just nitpick the bad, but rather, see the good. If you focus on the problem, the problem expands. If you focus on the solution, the solution manifests. If you think your partner could be better, be better yourself.

4. **Defensiveness and the Need to be Right**

Do you often defend your point of view and feel the need to constantly be right? Yeah, I get it—we all do to some degree, but keep your ego out of it. When you're wrong, admit it. Would you rather make your point and be "right" or leave it lay and be happy? Sometimes, you have to surrender and just say sorry for the misunderstanding or miscommunication. Don't let petty problems fester, as they are often not worth it. Time spent angry is time wasted.

If you are doing any of these things in your relationships, stop. Change your bad habits.

Everyone says there are plenty of fish in the sea, and I agree—there are. Trust me, I used to be an avid fisherman. But that gets old. I am now in a loving relationship and have no interest in looking back. Of course, we still have our stuff. But usually, when there's an issue, I can trace it back to the lack of energy we are putting into our relationship or the way we are falling victim to one of the 4 above-stated unhealthy habits that destroy love.

When we get complacent and stop spending quality time together, doing the little things like coconut oil massages and making each other morning coffees, tension arises. So keep putting in the energy and enjoy abundant love each and every day.

LISTEN

OBSERVE

VOICE

EMPATHIZE

REPAIR

L.O.V.E.R.

Next time you experience conflict with someone you care about, think about the acronym L.O.V.E.R. I know you may be thinking, "Oh, no, Cary! Not another acronym!" But the reason I love acronyms and frameworks is that they stick! They're easy to remember. So when tension arises, try this step-by-step process to de-escalate any situation with your significant other, your extended family, your friends, or even in the workplace with your co-workers.

- **Listen** to what the other person is saying and truly hear why they are upset. The question "How do you feel?" or "What is going on?" can lead you to uncover the truth. Just make sure the beginning of your sentence doesn't interrupt the middle of theirs.

- **Observe** their body language and facial expressions (55% of communication is non-verbal)[1], then recognize if their body language matches what they are saying or if you need to dig deeper. "I'm fine…" spoken with clenched fists might need a reassessment.

- **Voice** your side of the situation in a calm and collected manner. Don't react with emotion, but rather respond with logic. Make sure your facial expressions and body language are synergistic with the words coming out of your mouth.

- **Empathize** with their perspective and understand where they are coming from. Repeat their problem in a statement such as, "I understand you are frustrated because… and I totally get it."

- **Repair** the situation by creating a win-win for everyone involved. Think honestly about what would result in a peaceful resolution, and proceed with a plan to do just that.

This exact talk track has helped me countless times with my wife, family members, friends, and my team whenever a situation arises. And it can help you too. Next time be a L.O.V.E.R. and Happy Hustle past adversity with ease.

THE LOVE CALENDAR

I'm sure you have heard of Pareto's Principle, the rule of 80-20. Basically, 80% of your desired output is derived from 20% of your input. Well, in your relationship, I have a similar theory: I believe if you are happy in your relationship 80% of the days in a month, then you should continue forward with your partner.

Now, that leaves room for the occasional blow-up and drama, but it should only make up a small fraction of your time together. This is a tactic I've used in my relationship with great success. My wife and I call it the Love Calendar.

Basically, you create your own internal rubric to assess your daily love number, scoring 1-10. We like to use a whiteboard calendar and hang it in our bedroom. Every evening, I ask my wife, "What was your love number today?" A score of 10 would mean tons of passion, joy, love, and sex. Obviously, a 1 would be the opposite, meaning a day full of deep despair and arguments, with no love or connection.

If your partner says 9 and you say 7, then write the average (8) on the calendar for that day. If the score is 5 or greater, it is a love day and you then draw a heart around the number on the calendar for that day. If the average of your two numbers is below 5, then you draw an X over the number on the calendar. This gamification can make a huge positive impact on your loving relationship, as it has on mine. As you already know from The 10 Alignments, it's helpful to see and quantify things in our lives. *Again, what you measure you can manage.*

♥ LOVE CALENDAR ♥

SUNDAY	MONDAY	TUESDAY	WEDNESDAY	THURSDAY	FRIDAY	SATURDAY
1 8	2 4	3 6	4 9	5 6	6 10	7 9
8 5	9 6	10 8	11 10	12 7	13 4	14 6
15 8	16 10	17 3	18 9	19 8	20 9	21 6
22 8	23 4	24 9	25 6	26 10	27 8	28 5
29 7	30 6	31 8	1	2	3	4

SCORE: 25 HEARTS of 31, 80% LOVE!

PRO TIP: Keep the calendar in your bedroom, and at the end of the month, assess how much love there was. If only 50% of the days were marked as love days that month, y'all have some work to do. It may even mean you want to reconsider the relationship entirely if this is a consistent theme month over month. If the calendar is 80% chock-full of hearts, awesome! You are in a healthy, loving relationship, so keep on keepin' on, baby! Download the Love Calendar template at thehappyhustle.com/hub.

LOVE JOURNAL

Another tactic to foster more love in your relationships is to write down one thing you are grateful for in your partner every single day. Steph and I use a journal specifically for daily gratitude, and we each have a section where we write whatever comes to mind that we are grateful for about one another on that particular day. You don't have to share it with them right away, or ever. But, you can if you'd like. By doing this, you'll start looking for new things to be grateful for as opposed to looking for things to nitpick.

See, we as humans possess a negativity bias, which is a tendency not only to register negative stimuli more readily than positive stimuli but also to dwell on these events. This means that we feel the sting of criticism more powerfully than we feel the joy of praise. Hence why it's important to keep a Love Journal and look for positive things to be grateful for daily.

At the end of each month, you can give each other your list to read and enjoy the love that follows. At the end of the day, relationships require consistent effort. Like playing a professional sport, you must practice every day in the dark in order to be the best you can be and shine in the light. If you want to crush it come game time and get the W, it's not enough to just show up on game day or practice once a month.

LOVE IS EFFORT MULTIPLIED.

You must put in the work and Happy Hustle for your relationship and "practice" every day. Love is effort multiplied. Every day, in every way, put in the constant effort to care, support, protect, respect, communicate, trust, and honor your significant other. Then, enjoy the results.

LOVE YOURSELF

It's time to really love and appreciate who you are. If you don't currently feel that love for yourself, then it's time to become who you want to love. You have to be able to wholeheartedly love yourself before you are able to truly love others. You may have heard this before, but it is so very true. Being in a place of inner peace & love attracts others into our lives who are in similar states. That is when unconditional love can manifest. That is when you inadvertently invite your "soulmate" into your life.

Back in my early 20s, I serial dated aka "played the field" frequently. Sure, I enjoyed the chase and challenge. But I was truly in a state of insecurity and searching for something I wasn't ready to find. Even when I was in a relationship, I was never fully able to commit and shed all of my layers.

Protecting myself in nearly every aspect, I was not in a place to entirely give to the individual, regardless of how great she was, for I had not yet fully given to myself. Being content with yourself will help to bring you the inner Zen needed to attract and find a desirable counterpart to share your journey with. Once I found myself in this place of peace & self-love, the universe provided me with exactly what I was searching for and more. And it will do the same for you.

When you start to live this way, you start to love yourself more. When you love yourself, you attract love from others. Without that self-love, finding a counterpart becomes an arduous endeavor. When we truly are at peace inside and love ourselves fully, we open ourselves up to love from others. We don't necessarily have to be content with our current career situation, housing situation, how much money we have in the bank, or where we are in life. But, we do need to accept the circumstances and love ourselves regardless. If we are genuinely seeking love, we must first search within.

Practicing self-love is a part of Happy Hustlin'. It's all about giving ourselves care and affection first and foremost, similar to the airplane spiel the stewardess goes through in their pre-flight routine. In case of an emergency, they instruct every passenger to put on their own oxygen mask, before assisting others. This is true for love and life. You are unable to help your loved ones or the person next to you if you cannot breathe yourself. You have to love yourself first. Be kind to yourself. Make strides to consciously be aware of your inner thoughts and your mind's chatter. Fill yourself with goodness, positive self-talk, and powerful affirmations. Then, you can share that love and kindness with others.

YOU HAVE TO LOVE
YOURSELF FIRST. BE
KIND TO YOURSELF.
FILL YOURSELF
WITH GOODNESS,
POSITIVE SELF-
TALK, AND POWERFUL
AFFIRMATIONS.
THEN, YOU CAN
SHARE THAT LOVE
AND KINDNESS
WITH OTHERS.

LOVE OR FEAR

It is said that every action stems from two basic emotions: love or fear. When we are consciously aware, we can choose clearly. When we operate out of fear, we often are coming from a place of lack, angst, insecurity, or stress. Instead of giving into fear, choose to operate out of love in all of your relationships. I know it sounds woo-woo, but hang in there.

Once we are grounded, steadily breathing, and loving ourselves, we can then give from our overflow. We can give away the excess love and kindness we possess. The heart is the strongest muscle in the body, physically and emotionally. It's so emotionally strong that it can generate enough love to embrace everyone. Whether with a first-time interaction or a long-time lover, we possess the incredible aptitude to love without restraint.

LIFE IS ABOUT LOVE. GIVE IT, RECEIVE IT, AND ACTIVELY BE IT.

Begin to recognize love and give it more freely. Allow love to be the reason behind what you do, both personally and professionally. Love your prospects more, and watch your sales skyrocket. Love your team more, and witness increased productivity. Love your clients more, and create raving fans who positively promote you. Develop actions based on that feeling of goodness you can create. Be caring, compassionate, and kind. In all of your relationships, whenever you have an opportunity, share your loving kindness with others and witness the good karma of the universe circulate around you.

I'm advocating for the simple act of being kind with no alternative agenda. Hold the door open. Pick up a piece of litter. Carry someone's bag. Give a bonus to your assistant. Offer a generous discount to your clients just because. These minor actions often spring from love. Each day, incorporate loving micro-tasks. Be that person who exudes kindness and leads with love, not scarcity

& fear. Be open to receiving the light. Be conscious of your choices, whether they are made from love or fear. Whenever possible, go out of your way to be nice. Implement love-oriented micro-tasks each day and notice the change in the world around you.

Life is about love. Give it, receive it, and actively be it.

⊚ ALIGNMENT TAKEAWAY

The grass may look greener on the other side, but it often isn't. The grass is greener where you water it! Care for, fertilize, water, maintain, and enjoy your own grass…and don't worry about anyone else's.

In relationships, we can compare and despair ourselves to others. We see Joe Schmo and Cindy Lou Who post all of their extravagant vacays and date nights on the 'gram. We think to ourselves, "Why isn't my relationship like that?" Well, it could be, if you take 100% accountability!

Fire's still burning…

If you want your Loving Relationship score to be a 5 consistently, take full responsibility. Stop doing the 4 things that destroy love: Lack of Trust, Disrespect Towards One Another, Criticism or Judgement, Defensiveness and the Need to be Right. Deescalate issues using the **L.O.V.E.R. (Listen, Observe, Voice, Empathize, Repair)** talk track. And start giving your loving relationships the effort & attention they deserve. **If you want a 10, BE a 10.** Lead by example, and they will come around. More often than not, they will recognize your extra efforts and rise to the occasion. Happy Hustle your Loving Relationships, as love is truly what life is all about!

☑ DAILY ACTION TASKS TO HAPPY HUSTLE:

Loving Relationships

1. Send a gratitude text or video message to one person you care about.

2. Give a gift to someone who deserves it.

3. Surprise your lover with an act of service.

 PRO TIP: Fill out the Perfect Partner Page. You can download the FREE fillable PDF version at thehappyhustle.com/hub.

Whether you're happily married or single and looking for love, this exercise can help! Create **"The Perfect Partner Page"** where you write in extreme detail exactly who you want to attract; the more detailed, the better. Get out a piece of paper or your note-taking device and identify the following in your Perfect Partner:

- **Personality Traits** (Overall vibe, what type of person they are)

- **Looks** (Height, weight, body characteristics, eye color, hair color, shoe size, etc.)

- **Style** (How do they dress and show up?)

- **Sense of Humor** (Funny, jokester, good sport, etc.)

- **Interests** (What draws their attention?)

- **Hobbies** (Sports, art, martial arts, etc. What do they like to do?)

- **Morals** (The core values they stand behind)

- **Faith** (What do they believe in?)

- **Profession** (What do they do for work?)

- **Family** (What's their family like? Mom, dad, brothers, sisters, etc.)

- **Kids Preferences** (How many? Boys, girls, both?)
- **Location** (Where are they from?)
- **Political Views** (What is their political stance?)
- **Conflict Resolution** (How they handle conflict)
- **Long-Term Vision/Goals** (Who they want to become and what they wish to accomplish)
- **Anything else you can think of** (Seriously, go deep.)

You must first get clear on who exactly you want to attract in order to manifest it. Even if you're in a relationship, have your partner go through the exercise with you, and each create your Perfect Partner Page. Then, if you feel called, respectfully share it with one another, generating transparency on a whole new level.

Then, you can each work to become the partner one another's soul seeks. I know it seems a bit of overkill. But I'm telling ya, spend the time, write this out, and watch yourself manifest the Perfect Partner! Just like shooting a bow & arrow, you have to identify the target before you can hit the bullseye!

In the meantime, if you are single and manifesting your perfect partner, I recommend limiting the time spent dating or hooking up with those you know aren't a good fit. Conserve & protect your Qi (energy). Focus on becoming the best version of yourself.

😄 EMBARRASSING FUN FACT

Before meeting my wife, I was practicing abstinence. I just came off a bender in Southeast Asia and needed time to focus on myself. And wouldn't you know it, after a couple of months of practicing pure self-love and creating my Perfect Partner Page, I connected with the love of my life!

🧠 POWERFUL RESOURCES

Books:

The 5 Love Languages by Gary Chapman

The Mastery of Love by Don Miguel Ruiz

The 7 Principles for Making Marriage Work by John M. Gottman, Ph.D

Podcasts:

Oprah's *Super Soul*

The Happy Hustle™ Podcast Episodes #323 with Genevieve Pleasure; #369 & #409 with Intimacy Expert Susan Bratton (very juicy); and #46, #114, & #160 with Steph

Movie:

The Notebook

Online Course:

Legado Family—A program designed to help you create and secure your family legacy and values, designed through symbols, traditions, doctrine, defining events, and structure. Highly recommend it. This course was created by Rich Christiansen, a true Happy Hustler, successful serial entrepreneur, loving husband, and dedicated father to 5 sons. Fun fact: each of Rich's sons started their own prosperous 7-figure business in their teens then donated the profits to charity as a rite of passage at the age of 18.

HAPPY HUSTLER SPOTLIGHT 🔦

Randy Garn

When I think of one of the world's greatest Happy Hustler's I know, I think of my friend Randy Garn. Not only is he a *New York Times* bestselling author, Ernst & Young Entrepreneur of the Year, and Harvard Business alumnus,

but he is kind and empathetic with a loving family of 6 kids and a beautiful wife. Sure, he works closely with and advises some of the world's most recognized CEOs, companies, and thought leaders, but that's only a portion of why I wanted to spotlight him.

He is a man of faith who puts God & family first. He prioritizes the Loving Relationships in his life, starting with his amazingly talented wife and his 6 kids. He splits his time on his gorgeous 600-acre ranch outside of Jackson Hole, Wyoming, fly-fishing for monster trout in the summer, and heli-skiing fresh powder in the winter. He has his hand in multiple successful ventures and is connected to literally some of the most powerful and influential people in the world.

But one thing that really stood out to me when I interviewed Randy on *The Happy Hustle™ Podcast* (check out episode #295) is when he shared that he writes multiple handwritten notes to people he cares about EVERY SINGLE DAY. I mean, come on! That's amazing! Talk about an act to deepen the relationships in your life. Randy is a true Happy Hustler and an inspiration in my life. I am honored to call him a friend and share this spotlight with you in hopes that we can all, as Randy says, "Master the Art of Living."

PS: *Good luck finding Randy without a smile on his face! He is seriously always smiling and makes you smile as a result!*

CHAPTER FIVE

ALIGNMENT 5: MINDFUL SPIRITUALITY

Spirituality is the journey of seeking truth and wisdom through self-awareness, mindfulness, and inner exploration.

Wayne Dyer

As a part of a blissfully balanced life, you must incorporate Mindful Spirituality. I don't care what you believe in, but rather that you have faith in a higher power of some sort. So light an incense, rub a crystal, and flick on that salt lamp—we're going in!

I have been practicing and learning the ancient Daoist healing arts since childhood. My mom, who was big into Eastern medicine and methodologies, introduced me to Tai Chi, Qi Gong, Kung Fu, and the Daoist way.

I met a Traditional Daoist Priest, Master Wu Dang Chen at a very early age. When Master Chen was an impoverished child, he was chosen to be trained by 5 elder Daoist Masters in the sacred Wu Dang Mountain Temples. Through intensive training in this disciplined environment, Master Chen learned the art of mastering mind, body, and spirit. This training took him from his humble beginnings in rural China and led to him becoming a prominent spiritual leader in the West, having guided presidents, executives, and thousands of other people to help create health, happiness, and harmony in their lives.

I was 12 years old when Master Chen first called me his nephew and considered me as family. Up to that point, I would just sit in the back of the rooms at his lectures and workshops while my mom participated. I was always interested in martial arts, and casually trained, but never fully understood the meaning behind the methods.

I can distinctly remember the day when Master Chen came to my house to train my brother, Grant, and me. We began in the early afternoon by cultivating our Qi energy and learning basic Kung Fu kicks and punches. We continued to practice the same moves over and over again until we performed them to Master Chen's satisfaction. Grant became tired and bowed out of training as night fell, but I, hungry to learn this ancient wisdom and impress my Master, was a willing student far into the early hours of the morning.

Master Chen, Steph, and me at the Dao House in Estes Park, Colorado

Master Chen and I stayed up all night training, cultivating Qi, moving energy, being still, and recognizing our common affinity and connectedness. This night solidified my passion for martial arts. It also confirmed for me that there is a higher power—that we are spiritual beings, and that we must train our minds to connect to source energy.

Since then, I have been actively practicing various martial arts and stay regularly connected to Master Chen with frequent visits to his Dao House, a spiritual lodge and retreat center in the mountains of Estes Park, Colorado. Connecting to a higher power, I recognize the importance of Mindful Spirituality while Happy Hustlin'. It is something deep in my soul, and something I hope you do as well if you want true happiness and fulfillment on your journey.

"OBSERVE NATURE, OBSERVE YOURSELF, TEACH YOURSELF." MASTER WU DANG CHEN

SPIRITUAL BEINGS HAVING A HUMAN EXPERIENCE

Are you spiritual? Do you believe in God or a higher power? See, having a spiritual mindset is not exclusive to one religion or another. It is for everyone from everywhere. We can all tap into a higher power and even lean on it in times of adversity and triumph. Depending on where you scored yourself in Mindful Spirituality, this Alignment is going to help you create a deeper, more powerful connection to a higher power.

Let me first say, I believe in God—not one denomination or another, but a Divine Source. I grew up with a Catholic father and a Jewish mother. We didn't go to church religiously (pun intended), but when we did, we went to a non-denominational church called the Center for Positive Living, where I learned to believe in something greater than myself.

I also learned to love everyone from all religions, races, and cultural backgrounds. I learned to trust that everything happens for a reason and to understand and accept that we all have a purpose. I still mostly believe that; however, I take everything I learn, especially regarding religion, with a grain of salt. I pray every day and at nearly every meal, speaking my gratitude every morning and night for all that I have been blessed with. But what's important for me more than any particular religion is to simply have faith in a higher power and a strong moral compass. Having a spiritual mindset coupled with distinct values to stand behind allows me to vibrate at a higher frequency, and it can allow you to do the same.

In order to truly become a Happy Hustler, you must practice some form of mindfulness regularly. This is essential to achieve inner peace and balance, especially given the craziness of the modern world. We all need to take the time to tap into our higher selves and connect with a greater power.

Now, I could probably write a whole book on mindfulness and spirituality. Many others have, and some of my favorites are listed at the end of this chapter in the resource section. Instead, what I want to do here is cut straight to the chase and give you The Happy Hustle™ way to raise your spiritual vibration.

HAVE FAITH IN A HIGHER POWER AND A STRONG MORAL COMPASS.

Be Present

Some say there is no past and no future—only the eternal present. Life is about being the fullest expression of yourself in every moment. Do you suppress your true self depending on the environment and the people in it? Of course, you do. We all do.

LIFE IS ABOUT BEING THE FULLEST EXPRESSION OF YOURSELF IN EVERY MOMENT.

When we can own who we are and live unapologetically in the eternal present moment, only then can we Happy Hustle freely. We can appreciate the short seconds, that make up the minutes, that make up the hours, that make up the days, that make up our life. Tune into the present today.

It is a constant practice—I still have to judo chop myself back to the present moment on the reg. Being fully present is an ever-constant, lovingly fierce internal battle for all of us, never declaring victory, only advancing our position. Bottom line—be present in whatever you're doing.

Attitude of Gratitude

All of these concepts and practices will work to raise your spiritual vibration. However, without this key ingredient, your life is going to feel flat. If you want to Happy Hustle a blissfully balanced life of passion, purpose, and positive impact, develop an attitude of gratitude. That means actually changing your brain's biological response system.

DON'T WASTE ANOTHER MOMENT! FIND GRATITUDE FOR EVERYTHING YOU HAVE AND EVERYTHING YOU DON'T.

A National Institute of Health study[1] found that when you express kindness or feel gratitude, your hypothalamus floods your brain and releases dopamine and serotonin. These are the two crucial neurotransmitters responsible for our emotions, enhancing our mood immediately, and making us feel happy from the inside.

Don't waste another moment! Habitually instill gratitude into your everyday life. Find gratitude for everything you have and everything you don't. For example, if you have a roof over your head, food in the fridge, and reliable transportation, find gratitude, as the majority of the world's population doesn't. If you don't have any missing limbs or life-threatening diseases, find gratitude. Consciously identify and list what you are grateful for every day, big or small, and make it a part of your routine.

Seat of Character

The mental and moral qualities distinctive to you are what make up your character. The trick is to ride on a seat of character that positively reflects who you are and to do so consistently. Practice not allowing other people's pressures, intentions, or actions to dictate your decisions. Instead, choose to always operate with integrity that is true to you. I am definitely not perfect, nor do I claim to be. But I've changed my dishonorable ways from when I was a kid and now operate with full integrity. I always strive to do the right thing, even when it isn't the easy thing.

So whether you're at work or at home, or anywhere in between, let your clear morals be non-negotiable guidelines to Happy Hustlin' a life of integrity. You can then base your decisions, both personally and professionally, on these morals you live by. In life, your judgment will be questioned. You will have to make countless decisions between what is *right* and what is *wrong*. People will push you in different directions and attempt to influence and coerce you.

WITH INTEGRITY, LIFE IS SO MUCH BETTER.

I have operated with a lack of integrity in the past. And every time I did, I felt shame in my soul, like when I took something that wasn't mine or made a questionable business deal. Typically, by the time you recognize that you should have made a different choice, it is often too late—the deed is done.

But when I have made a mistake, I learned from it, apologized, took accountability, then moved forward as a better man. I now ride on my seat of character that reflects who I am and who I want to be, every day, as much as I can. With integrity, life is so much better.

Think about how you can reflect more closely on who you are and who you want to be by operating with character in each and every action. If you want to take it a step further, think about how you would want yourself to act 10 years from now. Act like—and be—that person today.

Alignment or Misalignment

Kevin Walton, a super enlightened friend of mine and creator of The Light Beings, a spiritual community, believes that life is an exploration of unlimited creative potential. It is not about being right or wrong, making mistakes or succeeding. Life is only about living in alignment or misalignment with your true self.

Wait, what? We've been complicating the crap out of life this whole time? Yep. I know when I first heard of this concept, my mind had a little explosion of awakening. I had previously been caught up with what I *should* be doing, achieving my goals, and measuring progress on the way. But, when I realized I was doing it all out of alignment, I had no choice but to kick myself in the proverbial gonads and change my ways. What are you doing that is out of alignment? Take a moment to really reflect. Then be brave and make a pivot if needed.

Meditation

Another way life can be Happy Hustled is with regular meditation. Meditation is vital to the mind, body, and spirit. It allows your soul to shine and your mind to rest. There is so much good that comes from meditating—no wonder so many of the world's ancient philosophers, successful leaders, entrepreneurs, athletes, and stars take time alone to find their inner Zen.

Let me preface this section by saying that I am far from a meditation expert. I haven't gone full monk mode for a year in Tibet...yet! I haven't done a 7-day solo silent retreat in a dark cave in the middle of California. I haven't even meditated every day since I started writing this book. Guilty. I miss a day here and there. What I have done, though, is notice how much happier and grounded I feel when I do meditate.

Take a moment now to reflect. Focus on nothing but your breath, and clear your mind as much as possible. Inhale deeply through your nose. Exhale fully through your mouth. For most, 6 deep breaths can change your state.[2] Do that now, and feel the shift.

There are many unique ways to meditate, so don't feel bad or wrong in your process. If your mind wanders in the midst of meditation, then congratulations! You're normal. Just gently guide your thoughts back to your breath and get back into that Zen-like state.

SLOW IT THE HECK DOWN, PARTNER, AND JUST CHILL IN THE STILL.

I enjoy meditating outside, in the mornings, either on the beach or in the wilderness, depending on where I am. It is an unbelievably beautiful and humbling way to start the morning. Being one with nature—the sun, the wind, the endless ocean, the vast mountains—helps put everything in perspective. If you don't live near the beach or mountains, just go outside and meditate in a quiet place; you'll be happier if you do.

C.I.T.S.

Listen, whatever you do, you owe it to yourself to have a stillness session in your daily routine. Slow it the heck down, partner, and just Chill In The Still. I like to remind myself daily to "C.I.T.S." my ass down. To just spend time every day reflecting, meditating, praying, or whatever it is that makes you slow down and connect with source energy.

Don't overcomplicate it. Just get still and quiet for 5-10 minutes and focus on your breathing. That's it! Just start with that. Of course, you can take it to higher levels and increase the duration, but even just that few minutes a day will make a huge difference on your Happy Hustlin' journey to blissfully balanced greatness.

 PRO TIP: Create I AM mantras for yourself to say during mediations.

Here is a brief outline of how I do it; fill in the blank with what speaks to you:

- I AM (an aspirational personal attribute).
- I AM (a long-term goal you desire to achieve).
- I AM (a philanthropic goal you desire to achieve).
- I AM (a financial goal you desire to achieve).
- I AM (an aspirational emotion or thought).

Then, you can train your subconscious self while meditating!

HAPPY HUSTLE

CHILL
IN
THE
STILL

Prayer

The power of prayer has been undeniable in my life. Prayer is conscious, personal communication with a higher power. A way to talk to God, if you will. I recommend not just praying when you need help or want something, but rather keeping the lines of communication open with daily check-ins. You don't have to be on your knees with your hands crossed in a church (although you can). You can pray everywhere: in your car driving to the office or at the gym on the treadmill or in bed before you go to sleep. The important thing is just that you do it.

Meal time is a trigger for prayer to me. I make sure to pray before just about every meal. I thank God for all of the blessings in my life and this nourishment for my body. I express gratitude during all of my prayers, and I feel that is a key piece. So give it a go now, even if just for 10 seconds. Pray to a higher power. Pray more, stress less.

Surrender The Soul

Learning how to surrender and find flow could be one of the more powerful habits to develop in your current reality. Instead of resisting what is happening for you (not to you), tensing up, fighting for your way or the way you assumed it should go down, try something else: surrender.

> **THE ONLY THINGS YOU CAN TRULY CONTROL ARE YOUR ATTITUDE, EFFORT, AND REACTION. DON'T STRESS OR WORRY ABOUT THINGS OUT OF YOUR CONTROL.**

Accept what is taking place and find gratitude for it. Whatever it is, surrender and flow. The only things you can truly control are your attitude, effort, and reaction. Don't stress or worry about things out of your control. Find the silver lining and learn from the experience while flowing with the river of life.

After traveling to the Temple of the Universe in Alachua, Florida, and meditating with the great Mickey Singer, I learned a lot about myself, life, and spirituality. Mickey Singer is a *New York Times* best-selling author of *The Untethered Soul* and *The Surrender Experiment*, and co-founder of what is now WebMD. He is one of the most unique and awakened beings I've ever met. He has a way of captivating a crowd with his charisma, often cracking jokes mid-meditation.

The Temple of the Universe is a yogi's heaven, with wide-open, beautiful rolling green hills, thick massive trees scattered throughout the property, birds chirping, and animals playing—a real old Florida feel. It's the perfect place to tap into oneself and the mind.

Stillness and calm exude over the 200+ acre property. The temple itself is a wooden cabin-like building built by Mickey himself back in the 70s with soft carpet flooring (where everyone sits), candles imperfectly placed throughout, and pictures of spiritual gurus hanging on all of the walls. Mediations and teachings are free, and he welcomes guests of all kinds for group meditations and teachings throughout the week at specific times. It is there where I first learned to *surrender*, and oh boy what a difference it makes!

Mickey said, in essence,

Think of your mind as a house. Many of us have a completely messy house. Oftentimes, this place is filthy, with dust in every corner, dirt on the floors, nothing is organized nor put away... I mean, stuff everywhere. Not to mention there are holes in the actual foundation and termites are rotting its core.

Ask yourself, how clean is your house? Do you have negative thoughts acting as termites eating away throughout your day? Do you stress yourself out about work or family drama that doesn't serve you? If someone cuts you off in traffic or honks at you, do you lose your cool? Think of all the melodramatic thoughts we put in our minds or what we create from nothing. All of these reactions and thoughts are reflections of our mind's state.

We have to clean it up and remove the obstacles. Much like we have to clean our actual houses, we have to clean up and provide some TLC to our mind and body, our Temple. We have to relax and release.

You can conquer your thoughts. You can keep your house clean. You can practice Mindful Spirituality while Happy Hustlin' on your journey, every step of the way.

Mickey Singer built a multi-million-dollar company all from his shack in the woods in the middle of Florida.

Steph and me at Mickey's Temple of the Universe

Be You, Be True

If you want to be a Happy Hustler, always be unapologetically yourself. All jokes aside, this is a game-changer. Being transparent and real are the most appreciated qualities in this world full of false digital identities. If you run a company, personal brand business, or are forward-facing in any capacity, this is especially HUGE. Know who you are as a human, what you stand for, what you stand against, and what you're willing to fight for. Know that your opinion of yourself is what matters most. And know that you will never regret being true to your soul. Plus, people will be far more likely to buy from you if they know, like, and trust you—hence the importance of being unapologetically yourself.

> **IF YOU WANT TO BE A HAPPY HUSTLER, ALWAYS BE UNAPOLOGETICALLY YOURSELF.**

Pre-game stretches at Miami Model Beach Volleyball on South Beach in my limited camo attire

There are many times when I do things that are wacky and out there, unapologetically me. For example, I used to compete in the Miami Model Beach Volleyball tournament every year. This tournament involves the top 12 modeling agencies in Miami going head-to-head, battling for beach bragging rights. My attire each year was themed and unique, but typically involved a speedo. One year I wore an American Flag Speedo, American Flag Vest, and American Flag visor to represent the ol' USA.

Another time, I wore a camouflage get-up including a camo speedo, camo neck bandana, and camo bucket hat. I was pretty much the only one out there, out of hundreds of the most beautiful models gathered, wearing anything of the sort, since the tournament provides sponsored attire & team uniforms to wear. The point is not to go out there and rock a speedo. Although, kudos to you if you do. The point is to just be you and give less effs about what other people think. As Sally Hogshead says, *Different is better than better.*

When I was growing up, I remember how embarrassed I felt when I would be out with my mom at a restaurant and a live band started playing. She would always be the first one on the dance floor, not caring what people thought. She would light up the place with her 70s dance moves and natural glow. I honestly didn't start appreciating the self-confidence she demonstrated time and time again until I was much older. She was not trying to impress anyone. She was just having fun and being unapologetically herself.

Life Can Be Short

Life can be short, as I almost found out when I passed out, gashing my head open on the way down, and nearly died in April 2022 from extreme carbon monoxide poisoning. So here's what went down.

After a recent surgery, my dad received a call from a nurse during her routine checkup (first sign of a divine intervention), and she realized something was wrong and called 911 to his ranch house.

Emergency services came and rushed him to the hospital in an ambulance. He ended up being admitted for three days.

As soon as I got the call, I hit the road and drove for six hours from Missoula, where I was shooting a movie with my wife, Steph. I made it to Billings pronto and stayed near the hospital to keep tabs on my dad.

Then, my siblings, Grant and Megan, did everything they could to get on the next flights to Montana. We were all there to support my dad.

That night, after we left the hospital, the three of us headed to my dad's ranch house to crash. We planned to go back to the hospital in the morning since my dad had a heart procedure scheduled. We grabbed some leftover soup from the fridge, cozied up by the fire, and watched a movie. I was the last one to hit the hay, making my way upstairs where Grant and Megan were already sound asleep.

Around 3 AM, our 15-year-old pitbull, Biggie Smalls, went bonkers, barking nonstop. I jumped out of bed, rushed downstairs, and let him and our other two dogs, Ninja and Zadie, outside.

Now, here's where things get absolutely insane. I shut the glass door, and the next thing I remember is smashing my head against it, gashing my forehead, and waking up on the floor. Blood was pouring out, and I was completely disoriented, with a pounding headache like I'd never experienced before.

I woke up to the dogs barking to get back inside, laying nearly lifeless on the floor next to the door, and let the dogs back in. I stumbled to the nearest bathroom, which, coincidentally, is close to the new heater my dad had "professionally" installed the week before. I remember lifting the toilet seat to take a leak, and that's the last thing I recall. I blacked out and collapsed, unconscious again, right there on the bathroom floor.

I can't even express how grateful I am for my incredible dog, Ninja, a Belgian Malinois/German Shepherd Mix. He woke me up from that unconscious state by licking my face and whimpering loudly over my body. My sister also passed out in the other bathroom, biting through her tongue and hitting her head as she fell unconscious. Fortunately, my brother, whom we woke with all the commotion, had the wherewithal to get us outside.

Let me tell you, it was one of the craziest nights of my life. We all ended up spending the entire next day in the ER. And you know what caused all the chaos? Carbon monoxide poisoning! Apparently the new heater that was recently installed was leaking massive

amounts. The poison was running through my bloodstream at death-defying levels, and those furry heroes saved us.

I'm just so blessed to be alive. The fire department said the carbon monoxide levels in that house were off the charts, the highest they'd ever seen with living people inside. It's a wild story, but let it serve as a reminder to check all your carbon monoxide alarms! And as it turned out, my dad's heart attack was caused by carbon monoxide poisoning, something they didn't

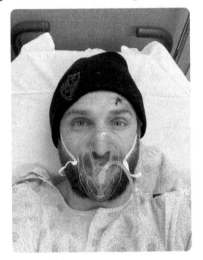

In the hospital with deadly levels of carbon monoxide in my blood stream. Close call indeed!

initially check for. They stopped his heart procedure and implemented an alternative treatment plan. We are all still recovering from the neurological effects, struggling daily with headaches, tremors, and vertigo as a result, but we are oh so grateful to be alive.

The point is, this experience truly made me believe in a higher power on a whole new level. I know angels and God were watching out for my family and me. Life is precious and can be short, so don't waste a second trying to be anyone but yourself. Live fully as YOU, without regrets. Meditate, have faith, and employ a spiritual mindset. Oh, and get a dog (bonus if they are a rescue)! Life's better when you do.

ALIGNMENT TAKEAWAY

Now, I don't expect an ancient Kung Fu Master, Daoist Priest, or Spiritual Guru to come to your house to explore these lessons with you. But I do want to stress the absolute importance of implementing some type of Mindful Spirituality practice regularly in which you connect to a higher power in your life, and having faith and morals by which you live.

LIVE FOR SOMETHING MORE THAN YOUR PERSONAL DESIRES.

I am a student of life. All religions are, thus, another lesson in the curriculum. In order to Happy Hustle a life of Blissful Balance, we mustn't overlook the essence of our spirituality. Believe in something greater than yourself. Live for something more than your personal desires. Remember, to **C.I.T.S. (Chill In The Still)**. Mindful Spirituality can exponentially increase your happiness and fulfillment along the journey, so make it a priority, my Happy Hustlin' friend!

DAILY ACTION TASKS TO HAPPY HUSTLE:

Mindful Spirituality

1. Chill in the still, meditate & focus on your breath for 10 minutes.

2. Write out 5 things you're grateful for in the morning and at night.

3. Pray. Communicate with a higher power, then listen in silence for the message you receive.

😆 EMBARRASSING FUN FACT

I often practice moving meditations with my katana sword in somewhat public places. Slicing old fruit and vegetables with swift swings is among my favorite simple joys. This often begets awkward looks from passersby and neighbors...with the occasional police questioning.

Me and my fruit splitting katana... you may be saying "Wow, two shirtless split pictures in one chapter, Cary? Bravo, sir, but questionable."

🏋🧠 POWERFUL RESOURCES

Books:
Become the Master Within by Master Wu Dang Chen
The Power by Rhonda Byrne
Conversations with God by Neale Donald Walsch
The Power of Now by Eckhart Tolle

Podcasts:
Podcast University with Jon Gordon
The Happy Hustle™ Podcast—Episode #59 with Master Chen

Movie:
Rewired with Dr. Joe Dispenza

Online Course:
Living from a Place of Surrender: The Untethered Soul in Action by Mickey Singer

HAPPY HUSTLER SPOTLIGHT

When I think of one of the world's greatest Happy Hustlers, I think of Oprah. Not only is she a multi-billionaire media mogul, author, actress, and philanthropist, but she is kind, empathetic, and deeply spiritual.

Throughout her career, Oprah has openly expressed her spirituality and its significance in her life. She believes in the power of connection, mindfulness, and the importance of living with intention. Oprah sees spirituality as a path of self-discovery and personal growth, and she has shared her insights with millions of people through her television shows, interviews, and books.

On an episode recorded for her *Super Soul* podcast, Oprah told Mickey Singer this about his book *The Untethered Soul*, "It's one of the most important books of my spiritual growth and development." Oprah says she doesn't even know how many copies she's gifted over the years—the number is just too high.

Her spiritual journey has led her to explore various philosophies and teachings, integrating them into her own unique perspective. Oprah's commitment to Mindful Spirituality has played a crucial role in shaping her values, promoting compassion, and inspiring others to seek inner fulfillment and purpose while Happy Hustlin' a life they love.

CHAPTER SIX

ALIGNMENT 6: ABUNDANCE FINANCIALLY

If you make meaning, you'll make money.

Guy Kawasaki

I've generated millions of dollars in revenue, selling both my own products and services and others', but there is one deal that I will never forget. I once closed a $25,000 sale on roughly a 45-minute Zoom call while sipping fresh coconut juice and sitting on a remote beach with my lovely then girlfriend, now wife (and baby momma), beside me in a sexy red bikini.

I was in a rural surf town, somewhere in the middle of Guatemala, where the Wi-Fi was surprisingly strong. I had always dreamed about laptop-lifestyle entrepreneurship, and here I was, truly living it: traveling, experiencing different cultures, eating unique foods, practicing other languages, meeting amazing people, and working from wherever I happened to be. I was making money and a positive impact while truly enjoying the journey. And nope, I wasn't asleep and dreaming! I was 100% awake and systematically harmonizing ambition and well-being! Aka Happy Hustlin' a blissfully balanced life!

I TRULY BELIEVE KNOWING HOW TO SELL IS A SUPERPOWER.

On this particular day, I had a handful of calls scheduled from inbound leads and began to work my way through each call using my proprietary sales process, R.O.A.D.M.A.P., which I'll break down for you a little later in this chapter. But in a nutshell, it took me just under an hour to build rapport with this one particular client, then determine his true obstacle, identify his real aspiration, demonstrate social proof and what's possible for him, qualify then match him with the right offer, ask him for the sale while utilizing ethical scarcity & urgency, and then finish it all off by pulling (not pushing) him into an opportunity to join our biohacking health and performance optimization coaching program. He was all in, said yes on the spot, and wire-transferred the funds immediately.

I truly believe knowing how to sell is a superpower. If you want to Happy Hustle in any capacity, making money has to be a part of the conversation. And sharpening your sales sword is one of the most efficient ways to do it.

Steph and me hanging poolside at our Guatemalan pad, living that location-independent entrepreneurship lifestyle

In the coming pages, I'll give you a crash course on how I went from $16K in student loan and credit card debt back in my early twenties to being debt-free and having $20K in savings *in less than 12 months*!

I'll provide you with the resources I used and still use today to live a financially abundant life—while not usually working more than 20 hours a week—and living a blissfully balanced life all the while. Buckle up, we're going in!

HAPPY HUSTLIN' FINANCIAL ABUNDANCE

Money, money, moneyy, moneeyyyy….. money! Yes, the lyrics from the classic song, "For the Love of Money" by The O'Jays were pretty spot-on. Some people do good things with money; some people do bad things with it, but everybody's got to have it.

As a Happy Hustler, I see money as a tool to help me live a life of passion, purpose, and positive impact. Depending on how you scored yourself in this Alignment, you're going to want to pay super close attention to this section, as money is essential if you truly wish to become a Happy Hustler and live blissfully balanced.

> ## IN A WORLD WITH INFORMATION READILY AVAILABLE AT YOUR FINGERTIPS, BEING FINANCIALLY IGNORANT IS A CHOICE.

The ability to financially provide for your family and loved ones is a universal goal. And being able to buy and invest in what you want, when you want, where you want is the ultimate financial freedom, right? Achieving financial freedom and abundance boils down to having and applying financial literacy, in my opinion.

Do you spend more than you earn? Do you invest in assets that appreciate or depreciate in value? Do you leverage bank accounts, credit cards, mortgages, government tax codes, and "the system" to your advantage? Or, maybe not so much… In order to be a Happy Hustler, you need to have your finances in check and educate yourself. So let's get into it.

IGNORANCE IS A CHOICE

First and foremost, let me say that in this day and age, in a world with information readily available at your fingertips, being financially ignorant is a choice. If you don't know the difference between a stock and a bond, what your credit card APR is, or the sales tax on every purchase you make, it is only because you have chosen not to educate yourself. That ends today.

It is time to become financially literate and optimize your finances. Buy financial books, subscribe to financial YouTube channels, listen to financial podcasts, and read financial blogs. You have the power to change your financial future, and it starts with education. The goal is to learn, create, and implement a foundational system that will work for you for the rest of your life with only minor adjustments along the journey as needed.

SPEND SMART

You must learn to spend your hard-earned money smart. There are certain things I don't think twice about spending money on, like books. I buy books the instant I am interested in one, as I know the value of that book's information could far outweigh the value of the money I pay for it. The same goes for health-optimizing items, like my gym membership, organic food, drinks, and vitamins—all steady green-light purchases. I know that by exchanging the paper (money) for the product, the transaction has exponential long-term benefits, so I don't spend mental capital (pun intended) overthinking the purchase.

However, there are other items I research, analyze, price shop, and compare before even thinking about actually pulling the trigger. And I don't just mean the big-ticket item purchases; it's also other less tangible things like investments in private contractors for my business, specific tech products, and dividend stocks.

Depending on the product, I will determine if it is a *need* or a *want* and if that money is better served elsewhere. I encourage you to put everything you wish to purchase through that filter. *Do*

I actually need it to enhance my happiness, health, business, or overall well-being? Or is it just a want?

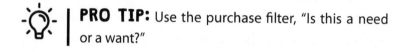

PRO TIP: Use the purchase filter, "Is this a need or a want?"

Now, I'm not saying don't treat yourself. Heck, I take pleasure in a new outfit and appreciate a gourmet dinner out just as much as the next person. But, until you have your finances in check and a system working for you where you actually know your numbers (ie: weekly budget, automatic investments, debt payoff plan, monthly bills, savings gameplan, etc.), keenly evaluate all of your purchases.

Once you have financial stability and abundance, you can set aside a percentage (I like 10%) of your income to spend on yourself, and then you can do so guilt-free.

Until then, keep in mind that every dollar spent now could be worth two dollars tomorrow. The Money Value Over Time (MVOT) is a real calculation that you must consider. With inflation, opportunity cost, and MVOT, each dollar you spend costs you more than you actually think. Without going too deep into the weeds here, just recognize that you must spend smart if you wish to achieve financial abundance.

SAVE SMART

Saving money every month is not only a solid idea, but it is also a necessity in order to become financially free. Even if you just set up your main bank account (I use Capital One) to deposit 10% of your income every month to your separate savings account (I use Ally Bank savings), and 10% of your income to your brokerage account (I use Charles Schwab), the power of compound interest over time will be quietly working in the background. Compound interest is

---

when you consistently make money on the interest accrued on your money. It's amazing! Put it to work for you ASAP!

They say the best time to start saving was 10 years ago, but the second best time is today. Start now! Even if you feel you don't have the liquid capital to save thousands, save hundreds instead. If you can't save hundreds this month, skip the dinner out and morning coffee, and save $50. If possible, create multiple savings accounts: one emergency fund (just in case), one retirement fund (for you as an old-timer to enjoy), and one personal savings (for investments, houses, cars, business, etc.). Save today, and free your future self. You won't regret it.

INVEST SMART

Investing is a whole other animal than simply saving. It's said the 3 main ways to achieve true wealth, not just get rich, are to:

1. **START A SUCCESSFUL BUSINESS.**
2. **BUY REAL ESTATE ASSETS AND LEVERAGE THEM EFFECTIVELY.**
3. **INVEST WISELY IN THE STOCK MARKET.**

I'm not a financial guru by any means, nor do I claim to be, but I have been able to take what I've learned and successfully invest in the stock market, real estate, and businesses. The major mindset shift I made was taking accountability for myself and my investments.

I didn't hire a financial advisor to manage my portfolio, although I have consulted with multiple. Instead, I vetted each potential investment opportunity, company stock, or real estate deal and made the investment decisions myself based on data and due diligence. For the most part, my initial investments continue to compound year over year. However, I play the long game, as should you when investing.

Many self-proclaimed financial experts don't know their ass from their elbow when it comes to predicting the market, so don't get duped. Most just make predictions and get lucky from time to time. With that being said, if you don't have the time to manage your own money, and you decide to go the financial advisor route, make sure to get personal references, and research the company they work for and which private interests they may be beholden to.

Now, there are some tried-and-true investment principles that can help guide your decisions. For one, invest in what you know. If you don't know anything about crypto or AI technology, it would be wise to educate yourself before investing in those sectors. Second, identify your risk tolerance. Know how much risk you can tolerate, and set operating standards based on that intel. I recommend reading two books that will help you become financially literate and better understand saving & investing.

- *I Will Teach You to Be Rich* by Ramit Sethi

  This is one of the best books I have ever read regarding money. It gives you a practical step-by-step system via a 6-week program that will transform your finances. He is also funny and shares tons of success stories from readers who have changed their lives by applying his teachings.

- *Money: Master the Game* by Tony Robbins

  Tony interviews some of the greatest minds in the financial and wealth management game. He gives actionable steps to investing, saving, earning, and much more. You will further understand the market and the proven and tested principles of investing.

AUTOMATE YOUR MONEY MACHINE

The real key to financial abundance is to automate your finances so that the system works while you sleep. The goal is to wake up on the first of the month and a series of digital events has taken place inside your accounts, allocating your money in the best possible way.

For example, you can eliminate the need to make a decision to save every month by simply setting up a recurring deposit to move money from your personal checking account into your savings account on the first of every month. I like to create recurring automation for my savings, investments, fun money, etc. to ensure long-term financial abundance. Make the smart decision once, spend the time to create the automation, and set yourself up for ongoing success.

It may take time to set up the automation, but it is more than possible—it is *essential* in order to Happy Hustle your dream reality. Read the books I have recommended above and implement the lessons ASAP if you want more Abundance Financially.

TAXES

Taxes are typically the single greatest expense of your lifetime. As the saying goes, there are two inevitable truths of life—death and taxes. If you want to have more money, focus on not only making more but keeping more! That means learning how to be proactive with your taxes, not reactive.

IF YOU WANT TO HAVE MORE MONEY, FOCUS ON NOT ONLY MAKING MORE BUT KEEPING MORE!

Your CPA can help make sure you are compliant and fill out the proper forms. However, if you're waiting until tax time to talk with them, you are reactive and will suffer the consequences. I recommended meeting with a tax strategist regularly throughout the year, thus being proactive, and then having them advise your CPA, bookkeeper, family office, etc. Now I am not a tax professional, but I do recommend seeking expert help in this area. My bro Garrett Gunderson is someone I look to for guidance. Check out his bestselling books and content to optimize your finances, thus, ethically decrease your tax burden.

USE TECHNOLOGY

Personal Capital is a solid web-based platform that allows you to see your financial well-being in its entirety. You can connect all of your accounts and credit cards so that you know your exact net worth, debts, etc. at any given moment. You can also create budgets and leverage many other solid features for managing your money. I highly recommend using this software to help keep your finances in check.

Acorns is an app that automatically invests and manages your money for you. You set the risk level and how much you want it to automatically withdraw from your checking account. Each withdrawal is allocated to your investments, and it does the work for you. You can also set it so that it rounds up a portion of every dollar you spend.

Quickbooks is a platform that you can use to track your business and personal finances. Knowing your numbers means not just checking them once a year come tax time. If you want to be financially abundant and free, know your numbers. Software like this can help.

I can't emphasize enough that when it comes to Happy Hustlin' your dreams into reality, money *has* to be a part of the conversation. Depending on where you ranked yourself in the Happy Hustler Assessment (1-5), take stock and prioritize change accordingly. You must educate yourself and become financially literate. I can tell you with certainty that if you don't have this Alignment in check, your entire existence will be filled with much more stress and anxiety.

Living in debt, paycheck to paycheck, coupon cutting, and price shopping may have been (or currently is) a part of your journey, as it was mine. However, it does not have to dictate your future financial success. Set up a system to spend, save, and invest wisely, and educate yo-self! Take full accountability for your current financial status. Learn from your past mistakes and make better financial decisions from this day forward. It's time to Happy Hustle that moolah, mi amigo!

I learned more about business and finances in the first 6 months of starting a company than I did in 4 years of college. Take accountability for your financial education. Here is a rare pic of my immediate family together at my college graduation.

THE POWER OF SALES

One of the quickest ways you can make more money right away is by learning effective sales techniques. Sales are the lifeblood of any business. Increase your sales, and you'll make more money. It's as simple as that.

One of the ways I was able to get out of $16K in credit card and student loan debt and amass over $20K in savings in less than 12 months in my early twenties was by sharpening my sales sword. I fully realize this isn't a business book per se, but in order to help you Happy Hustle your Abundance Financially, sales secrets must be shared. If you take away nothing else from this book but how to increase your sales, I know this will positively impact your life. *That is how important sales are to your success.*

HELP PEOPLE SOLVE THEIR PROBLEMS BY SELLING A SERVICE THAT TRULY ADDS VALUE TO THEIR LIFE.

I'm going to give you a quick crash course on some of the most successful sales strategies I used to sell millions of dollars while typically working less than 20 hours per week. And no, I'm not talking about slimy, scammy, hard-closing sales. I'm talking about actually *helping* people solve problems by selling a service that truly adds value to their life.

Whether you are selling online coaching, courses, books, live events, a physical product, a service, or something in between, these sales tactics will be applicable.

But first, I want to give credit where credit is due. I have learned some of the following sales tactics and strategies from my superb sales friends:

- Mr. Eli Wilde, #1 sales producer for Tony Robbins, who has sold over 9 figures at the time of this writing

- Mr. Randy Grizzle, OG salesman and founder of Closer Secrets, who sold over $25 million by phone for Russell Brunson and early-stage ClickFunnels (Check out Episode #11 on *The Happy Hustle™ Podcast* where I interviewed Randy on *Mastering your Money and High-Ticket Sales Process.*)

◦   Mr. Rory Vaden, *New York Times* best-selling author and Hall of Fame speaker, who also ran an 8-figure sales organization. (Check out Episode #42 on *The Happy Hustle™ Podcast* where I interviewed Rory on *Building an Influential Personal Brand*.)

Over the next few pages, I'll share with you some of the greatest lessons I've learned from these individuals. I'll also share a talk track I created for you to crush your sales meetings whether by phone, Zoom, or in person. I'll add in my own unique ninja sales kicks that I learned from selling myself as a professional model/actor on thousands of auditions. And as promised, I'll include the exact sales tactics I used from that beach in Guatemala to digitally close $25K+ sales in around 45 minutes, the same strategies I have successfully used many times since—and you will learn how you can, too. Saddle up—it's time for a sales rodeo!

#1 RULE OF SALES: LISTEN

Listening is legit your greatest asset as a salesperson. If you ask your prospect the right questions, they will give you the answers. All you have to do is listen. Don't overcomplicate this! Find out what they want by actually listening to them. Then, use their exact language and verbiage when presenting your offer to help fulfill their needs and get them their desired result. This should go without saying, but make sure you stand 100% behind whatever product or service you're selling or don't sell it.

PROFESSIONAL DECISION-MAKING HELPER

Let's face it, people need help making decisions. Be the facilitator of a conversation that guides your prospect into making the best decision for them, even if that decision means you will not close a sale. People get stuck in analysis paralysis and freeze. People will often procrastinate, especially when attempting to make a larger purchase. Your job as a salesperson is to be a professional decision-making helper. If you have your prospect's best interest in mind, you are going to substantially increase your sales closing percentage. Come from a place of integrity and service. I strive to sell to everyone as I would want my own mother or father sold to. Build a relationship with your prospect. Don't pressure them, but rather provide them with firm, direct questions to guide their decision. Indecision is thy enemy, so your goal is to get them to make a decision, be it a yes or a no.

EMOTION VS LOGIC

People buy with emotion but justify with logic. Therefore, you must appeal to their emotional state throughout the sales process by painting a picture of what is possible for them. Then, you must equally justify that with logical sense. This often means doing the math, showing them that X amount of dollars invested with you will equal a potential return on their investment of X amount of dollars. Always do the math and share the numbers. Make sure to mention the opportunity cost of not buying.

COMMISSION BREATH

You know that invisible, deal-killing stench that your prospect can smell from a mile away? That's commission breath, my friend. Basically, it happens when you are more incentivized by your commission as a result of the conversion than actually helping your prospect make the best decision for them.

Commission breath can manifest as being pushy, talking too much about yourself, or bragging heavily about your product or service, just to name a few. Now, I'm not saying you can't be motivated by the money, but the goal in any sales interaction should be creating a WIN-WIN.

If you want to make more money, freshen up with *service* breath instead. Truly serve your prospect by helping them make a decision that is best for them. I love telling prospects, "My life isn't changing 1% whether you buy or not, but I truly know yours will." This can catalyze a paradigm reposition and often shifts the smell from commission breath to service breath. Freshen up, amigo!

PRICE ANCHOR

Price anchoring can be one of the most effective tools in your sales tool belt if used properly. Essentially, the first price you'll want to disclose is the highest in your potential products or services you offer. And if you only have one offer, you'll want to create a high ticket price anchor offer (even if you don't plan on really ever selling it). For example, if I am attempting to sell a 25K group coaching program, I price anchor with a 100K 1-on-1 coaching program that is logically more valuable. I present the 100K offer first, thus then the 25K offer or subsequently anything I present next, is now in relation to the higher price point, making it appear more affordable. You can really go down the rabbit hole of pricing psychology (ie: look at Starbucks and their cup sizes/ prices as a micro example), but to spare you details, just implement a price anchor and witness your conversions increase!

BUILT-IN OBJECTION BUSTERS

Everyone has objections. Figure out what the 5 main objections are for your product or service. Throughout your pitch conversation, bake those objections in organically so you are naturally busting them. Often, objections come down to time, money, spouse or partner agreement, etc. However, people are resourceful, so if they really want what you're offering, 9 times out of 10 they can be helped to overcome even their deepest objections. Bust their objections early, and show them a way through.

RAPPORT

OBSTACLE

ASPIRATION

DEMONSTRATION

MATCH

ASK

PULL

Whether you are selling in person, on the phone, or over a video call, the R.O.A.D.M.A.P. $ales $trategy can be used to increase your sales conversion rate. Customize it for you and your business or use it as is. Just do not skip steps. Each step builds upon the other. Make sure to listen and take notes throughout your interactions. Here is the R.O.A.D.M.A.P. $ales $trategy I use every time I sell:

Step 1: Rapport
Start by finding out more about them. I like to ask, "Where ya from?" as people are often proud of their roots. Then I think about something positive I know about that place and share it. Give an honest compliment. Make small talk. Your first initial 30 to 60 seconds of the interaction will often dictate the overall vibe and, ultimately, the sales call success. Make a good first impression.

Step 2: Obstacle
Figure out what is holding them back. What are they struggling with? What is their weakness? What are they looking for help with? I like to ask, "What is the biggest challenge holding you back right now?" Find the pain in their life.

Step 3: Aspiration
Figure out what they actually want. I like to say, "So, paint the picture of your dream reality for me." Identify their dreams and aspirations and determine why they want what they want. This is crucial! Make sure you clearly understand this, as you will be using it later in the convo.

Step 4: Demonstration
Now that you know what's holding them back and where they want to go, you can clearly identify if what you have to offer is going to help get them there. If so, demonstrate their future success with your product or service. Use past stories of similar clients who have used your product or service and achieved results. People need case studies and social

proof to know what is possible for them. I like to say, "You remind me of (insert name of past similar client) and they were struggling with (insert similar problem) but then (insert success story)."

Step 5: Match

Before presenting the opportunity, you want to make sure this prospect is a good match for your product or service in order to ensure results. Don't skip this step. Make sure you are serving those you know you can get results for. That is how you will build word-of-mouth referrals. You should know your perfect target customer and sell to them specifically. I like to say, "Perfect fits for this (insert product or service) are people who are (insert traits of those who you wish to work with), does that sound like you?" If it's not a fit, or they don't qualify, walk away from the sale and be okay with that. Oftentimes, selling to the wrong type of clients just ends up causing more problems than it's worth.

Step 6: Ask

If it is a fit, make the ask. Present them with the opportunity to purchase your product or service. Frame the sale as a uniquely excellent opportunity for them to get results in whatever they are lacking or struggling with, and then congratulate them with genuine excitement. I like to ask the question, "Is there any reason you wouldn't take action and get started today?" If there are still objections, figure out what those are and how to alleviate them. I often like to bring up their dream and their pain points. I re-emphasize that it is possible to achieve that dream, and I am certain that the product or service will help them.

Step 7: Pull

This step can either be your greatest ally or your worst enemy. The key is to create ETHICAL scarcity and urgency. People often need a little pull in the direction of taking action. For example, you can give them the necessary incentive by offering only a limited number of spots in your program, offering only a limited quantity of products, or offering them a valuable bonus for signing up on the call. This step is crucial to closing the sale on the same day and avoiding the response, "I need to sleep on it," or, "Let me think about it and get back to you." I like to structure a three-hour window with my sales calls by stating, "I need a yes or no decision within three hours after our call ends in order to get you X bonus incentive or a spot in the program."

R.O.A.D.M.A.P. $ales $trategy is essentially the blueprint you can use to close discovery calls, in-person meetings, zoom calls, you name it. The steps are universal.

 PRO TIP: Check out The Happy Hustle R.O.A.D.M.A.P. $ales $trategy online course at thehappyhustle.com/hub for more in-depth training, videos, and resources!

ONE FINAL SALES NOTE: BE YOURSELF

One of the best ways I've found to actually sell myself and the product or service at hand is to be authentically me. You can only be authentically yourself, so keep it real and be transparent. People's BS meters are pretty sharp, and they can detect a snake in the grass. Don't be that person. Just Happy Hustle your sales in a way that you would want to be sold to yourself. Operate with respect and integrity, and you'll be on your way to Abundance Financially, my friend.

🎯 ALIGNMENT TAKEAWAY

So, there you have it. Sales are your escalator to Abundance Financially. Learn how to sell more effectively, and you can have it all in your life. Utilize the **R.O.A.D.M.A.P. $ales $trategy** on your next calls to guarantee an increase to your conversion rate. Financial freedom and abundance is more than possible for you. This is especially true if you follow the lessons in this chapter: spend, save, and invest wisely!

☑ DAILY ACTION TASKS TO HAPPY HUSTLE:

Abundance Financially

1. Send an email, text, DM, etc. to 5 potential prospects.
2. Create a video for a past client, adding value & offering support.
3. Read for 15 minutes from a financial book, article, or blog.

😆 EMBARRASSING FUN FACT

I've sold many things, and actually physically sold myself on multiple occasions. One time, immediately after watching *Magic Mike*, I thought I could hack it in Chicago as a bachelorette party dancer—Channing just made it look so fun and easy! Let me tell you, *it's not*. I'm not going to elaborate here, but let's just say things got...weird! That was the first and last bachelorette party I ever did.

💪 POWERFUL RESOURCES

Books:
Killing Sacred Cows by Garrett Gunderson
Rich Dad, Poor Dad by Robert Kiyosaki
Tax-Free Wealth by Tom Wheelwright

Podcast:
The Peter Schiff Show

YouTube:
Valuetainment by Patrick Bet-David
Magic of Finance by Andrei Jikh

Movie:
The Big Short

HAPPY HUSTLER SPOTLIGHT 🔦

Tony Robbins

Tony Robbins is not only one of the most influential human beings on Planet Earth, but he is for sure a Happy Hustler. Tony Robbins is an entrepreneur, *New York Times* #1 best-selling author, philanthropist, and the nation's #1 life and business strategist. For more than 4 decades, over 50 million people have enjoyed the warmth, humor, and

transformational power of his business and personal development events. I personally have been to multiple Tony Robbins seminars, including *Unleash the Power Within* and *Business Mastery*. I've read his books and listened to his audio programs. He has had a massive impact on my life and has inspired me on my journey.

In addition to selling out his own seminars and events, at the time of this writing, Tony is the chairman of a holding company of more than 50 privately held businesses with combined sales exceeding $6 billion per year. The guy knows the importance of financial literacy and creating a system that accrues wealth. And since he is financially abundant, he has turned to giving to others. He once said, "The secret to living is giving," which has stuck with me ever since.

Through his philanthropic partnership with Feeding America, Tony has provided over a BILLION meals to those in need. He has also initiated programs in more than 1,500 schools, 700 prisons, and 50,000 service organizations and shelters.

He has lived an extraordinary life and is a leader amongst leaders, coaching 3 US presidents, billionaires, Fortune 500 CEOs, professional athletes, musicians, actors, and everyone in between. I could go on and on about Tony's accomplishments. The point I want to make that is most relevant to this chapter is that he has his finances on point and seeks wisdom from those wiser than him regarding money. He invests regularly and has an automated system that grows his fortune while he sleeps. And you can too! He is definitely a Happy Hustler worth following, and I am grateful for all he has taught me.

CHAPTER SEVEN

ALIGNMENT 7: PERSONAL DEVELOPMENT

Formal education will make you a living. Self-education will make you a fortune.

Jim Rohn

I started my career in the entertainment industry like almost everyone else does—as a nobody. I didn't know one thing about the industry, nor did I really know anyone who did. But I did understand that personal development is the key to success in any industry—and in life. I used personal development to go from sketchy scams & Craigslist gigs to legit big-screen bookings and being repped by the top talent agency in the world. And you can use personal development to Happy Hustle your dream reality, too!

The key is to educate yourself. That means getting familiar with the industry language and the business's inner workings. Understand industry policy and processes. Research individuals who have achieved success in the industry and reverse-engineer their steps. And maybe most importantly, identify what can potentially hold you back and what skills can help you succeed.

BECOMING A WORKING PROFESSIONAL AND ACTUALLY GETTING PAID FOR YOUR SERVICES IN ANY INDUSTRY REQUIRES YOU TO FIRST BECOME A STUDENT OF THE GAME.

When I first dove into the entertainment business, I strived to learn everything I could. I sought a mentor who had been there and done that. I studied professionals who were at the top of their game and watched videos of them in action. I read books and articles about the industry. I networked with professional agents, casting directors, talent managers—heck, anyone who would talk to me. Becoming a working professional and actually getting paid for your services in *any* industry requires you to first become a student of the game.

When I was 16, I joined a talent agency in Florida. This particular agency hosted so-called "masterclasses" for potential new talent. After the class, they selected the individuals they wanted to represent—basically anyone willing to pay the $500 sign-up cost.

They counted on the newbies being so excited to be "chosen" that they'd hand over the cash with ease. Afterward, though, the agency never came through with marketing their talent nor with the jobs they promised to deliver.

That was my rude introduction to the industry and my first time getting ripped off by crooked agents. But it wasn't my last. (Side note: any agency that wants money upfront is a scam. Stay far away from them, even if they're promising lucrative gigs!)

After that lesson was learned and I ditched the agency, I started Happy Hustlin' the Internet for any modeling or acting jobs I could find in my free time to make some extra cash. I learned that doing test shoots with photographers would not only build my portfolio but would also help me become much more comfortable in front of the camera.

While I was in college in Chicago on my soccer scholarship, I answered a Craigslist ad that read "Looking for great male legs." I figured I had a shot since I played soccer basically all the time and had some pretty defined leg muscles, so I decided to submit some photos.

I actually came across that ad while I was sitting in my sophomore English class, and I was anxious to get my application in, so I left class and headed to the restroom to snap some calf selfies. You can imagine how awkward it was when another dude walked in and found that photoshoot going on!

To make a long story short, I submitted the photos and ended up booking my first paying job! It turned out to be a photoshoot modeling Crocs shoes—yes, those clunky, plastic fashionable clogs. There I was smiling, profiling, and flexing my calves in different pairs of Crocs' finest in exchange for $400! That was pretty decent coin for me at the time, so I splurged on beer and Taco Bell for all my college bros!

The funniest part was when the Crocs magazine came out, I eagerly tore through the pages in search of my glory shots, only to discover that all the images were from the waist down. Not exactly the claim to fame I was expecting!

I continued with my personal development in the industry when I decided to explore acting. I started with acting classes and then moved on to improv classes at the world-famous The Second City in Chicago, whose alumni include Steve Carell, Tina Fey, Amy Poehler, Jason Sudeikis, Mike Myers, and Chris Farley, to name a few.

WHATEVER YOUR GOAL, FIND A WAY TO PHYSICALLY PUT YOURSELF IN AN ENVIRONMENT CONDUCIVE TO LEARNING.

I dove all in, soaking up knowledge from each of the talented teachers. But I also took it a step further and volunteered to wait tables during the main stage and stand-up shows. My goal was to be around talented performers and watch the show for free, so I could learn from the best while on a budget. Whatever your goal, find a way to physically put yourself in an environment conducive to learning. It's a game-changer for personal development.

By the time I finished college and headed back to Florida, I had also gained modeling and commercial acting experience in Barcelona when I studied abroad. I had at least a dozen paid photoshoots under my belt and more than 3 years of acting and improv classes. I knew Miami had a strong market, so I did some research to find out the top agencies I should approach to get to the next level.

Wilhelmina was the top agency in Miami—and in the world, for that matter—with locations in over a dozen major cities. I did research ahead of time, learning about their director and bookers (team), the talent agency parameters, and their men's board details (online model database).

💡 | **PRO TIP:** Always do your research.

Usually, they don't take any walk-ins whatsoever, but with my printed picture portfolio in hand, I schmoozed the front desk girl to get my book (essentially a model's resume) passed back to the bookers.

One of the bookers who came out happened to be from Spain, and I did my best to charm him with my broken Spanish, recently acquired from studying abroad. Then, the director of the men's board came out, leafed through my portfolio, and offered me a 3-year contract on the spot!

A combination of luck, preparation, and creating opportunity—this was a massive accomplishment after a long and humbling journey in the industry, but it really was only the beginning.

I signed with Wilhelmina, but I later moved on to other world-renowned agencies

Baby face Cary in 3-piece suit action

and agents. However, the growth and learning lessons continued. For context, I used to go to over 100 castings per year and book roughly between 15-25 major jobs. That means I was getting rejected about 80% of the time!

So put yourself out there and don't be afraid to fail. Rejection is a part of business and life. It is said that the acting/modeling industry has a 97% unemployment rate. Literally, 9 out of 10 actors/models are NOT working on any given day. That means at times people in the industry must find other sources of income. Many turn to freelance promo modeling, brand ambassador work, and event catering. Hustlin' is the name of the game, and my experience in the industry has helped forged my resilient mentality.

Throughout my career, I hunted for my own jobs. I researched and dropped into casting directors' offices to meet with photographers and clients myself. I would bring cookies and a smile everywhere. Literally, I had multiple trays of cookies or other treats with hand-written notes ready to be customized to any given professional that I was attempting to network with. And it worked! I would often book the gig and found myself working more regularly thanks to these methods.

Although I look sad in this photo, I am actually super happy (and grateful) that I get paid to do things I enjoy with people I enjoy—aka Happy Hustlin'. Steph, my wife (pictured here), and I often still get booked to model/act together.

I continued to show up time and time again, knowing that it only takes one to make it worth it. For instance, one summer I ended up booking 3 SAG (Screen Actors Guild) national commercials: Home Depot, Corona, and Jeep. These netted me upwards of $20K for each commercial. $60K+ for technically 3 days of work! So the hard work can pay off quickly.

RESULTS WILL FOLLOW DEDICATED EFFORT.

After sharing the screen with stars such as Dwayne "The Rock" Johnson on the set of HBO's *Ballers*, working with directors such as Michael Bay on the set of *Transformers*, and doing dozens of national commercials, I learned a ton about the entertainment industry and myself. I still dabble as a part-time model and actor. It's now more of a casual, highly profitable side hobby, and I typically only accept fun, meaningful roles and bookings.

It's cool to look back on how far I've come; however, it definitely didn't come easy! Anything in life worth doing typically doesn't.

It takes time, relentless pursuit, and consistent persistency. It takes Happy Hustlin' and doing things others wouldn't, like embarrassingly bringing cookies to swoon casting directors and making cold calls to production managers, bypassing the middlemen. But if you're willing to work for what you want and can push through the rejection, you can have just about anything you desire. Just don't take no for an answer and stay steady in your pursuit of growth. Results will follow dedicated effort.

Whether you want to be a model or actor, a better entrepreneur or business professional, or you just want to become a greater version of yourself, personal development is the Happy Hustlin' way to achieve it. Think about what is required for success in your industry and how you can start developing and improving your skills today. Then, get after it!

THE 30–30–30 METHOD FOR GUARANTEED GROWTH

I hope the story of my journey in the entertainment industry makes crystal clear the sheer importance of learning something new every day. If you are not growing and evolving, you are shrinking and dissolving. I know it sounds dramatic, but we must prioritize our personal growth to be a true Happy Hustler.

IF YOU ARE NOT GROWING AND EVOLVING, YOU ARE SHRINKING AND DISSOLVING.

Where did you rank yourself in this Alignment (1-5)? If it's not a 5, then you have some room to improve. Heck, we all do. When you apply the following insights, this is one Alignment that can instantly have a positive effect. So, get ready to grow!

Do you have a plan or system in place to ensure your daily personal growth? Even if that is just reading 15 pages or listening to a self-improvement podcast, doing *something* every single day matters. It all adds up to consistent personal growth.

The fact is that all growth is rooted in skill acquisition. I know you have a ton on your plate—we all do—but that isn't an excuse to neglect yourself by failing to develop your skills. From learning copywriting to learning a new language, mastering sales to mastering speed reading, enhancing your verbal articulation to enhancing your EQ (Emotional Intelligence), each and every skill that you acquire adds value to your life.

You must make time to Happy Hustle for personal growth. This is neither a chore nor a burden. It's an absolute necessity, or else a life of meager complacency may be in your future. I created the *30-30-30 Method for Guaranteed Growth* that helps me ensure persistent personal development each day. Implement these elements into your routine every day to ensure ongoing personal growth. By the end of it, you will have added at least 90 minutes of personal growth into your daily routine.

HERE'S THE 30–30–30 METHOD FOR GUARANTEED GROWTH:

- **Morning** - Find 30 minutes of uninterrupted reading time for self-improvement, business, spiritual, or other non-fiction books. No, romantic novels don't count. Feed your mind with positive knowledge. Choose inspiring, educational content!

- **Afternoon** - Find at least 30 minutes of uninterrupted time to listen to a podcast or audio recording of your liking. Choose one that inspires, educates, and entertains you. Bonus points for finding one that is related to your specific goals. *Shameless Plug:* The Happy Hustle™ Podcast *is a solid personal growth choice!*

○ **Evening** - Find at least 30 minutes to watch a visually stimulating and educational show, documentary, or movie. I like going on YouTube for this and typing in self-improvement buzzwords. There is a ton of amazing content to choose from. So, just pick items that are relevant to you and your current goals. Change your habits from getting sucked into a meaningless television series to feeding your mind something of value. No more horror movies or crap content that doesn't add value to your life! Opt for content that raises your vibration and helps you grow.

These small changes over time will make a massive difference in your life. Leverage the compound effect. Start now by being extremely diligent with what you input into your brain. It all matters.

LEVERAGE THE COMPOUND EFFECT. START NOW BY BEING EXTREMELY DILIGENT WITH WHAT YOU INPUT INTO YOUR BRAIN. IT ALL MATTERS.

PRO TIP: If 90 minutes of personal development 7 days per week feels overwhelming, start with 15-minute blocks of time 5 days per week.

Use this time for reading, listening, and watching inspirational educational content. Then, you can build your way up by adding time accordingly. I want you to actually start implementing this practice into your routine, so better you start small than not start at all.

30–30–30 METHOD FOR GUARANTEED GROWTH

MORNING
30 MIN OF READING

AFTERNOON
30 MIN OF LISTENING

EVENING
30 MIN OF WATCHING

*All inspirational & educational content

INVEST IN YOUR PERSONAL DEVELOPMENT

Want to know the real catalyst to expedite your success? Hire experts. Want to learn how to do something in a fraction of the time? Hire a professional in that field. Set aside a budget each year to invest in your personal growth. That money can be used for attending conferences, hiring mentors or coaches, or investing in educational courses or training...and nothing else! Ask yourself these questions:

What skill could you acquire to help you expedite your success? Do some research and find someone who possesses that skill and pay them to teach you!

YOU ARE THE BEST INVESTMENT YOU WILL EVER MAKE.

What conference have you told yourself you should really attend next year? Purchase a ticket now. Don't delay. If money's tight, see if they offer a scholarship or if you can volunteer to work in exchange for entry. There's always a way.

What professional in your industry do you respect who is currently where you want to be? Do they offer a group coaching program or a 1-on-1 consulting option? If so, then reach out. Book a time to connect and see if it's a fit!

What course, training, or book could shortcut your learning curve in your business and help you spread your message to the world? Buy it! Don't hesitate.

Obviously, use discernment with any personal growth purchase as it seems everyone and their mother is a "guru" these days. My rule: I don't take advice from people I wouldn't honestly trade places with. During my vetting process, I extensively assess their life both personally and professionally. If I wouldn't want to be in their proverbial shoes, I find someone else to learn from.

Just know that *you* are the best investment you will ever make. Start taking this seriously. Happy Hustle your personal growth every single day. It may seem like the time, money, and resources could be better served elsewhere, but I promise you this is not the case. A dollar invested in yourself and your skill set today could be worth 3 dollars next week. Delayed gratification is the name of the game, my friend. Realize that investing in yourself will ensure that you are ready and able to seize future opportunities. It will help you create magic otherwise not possible without the tools you've spent years developing.

Me, with one of my mentors Russell Brunson—aka one of the best online marketers in the game and co-founder of the 9-figure company ClickFunnels—at his Inner Circle Mastermind in Boise

So get on with it, and make Alignment 7: Personal Development a daily priority!

THE HAPPY HUSTLE™ CLUB

As you now know, investing in yourself and surrounding yourself with a like-minded community is imperative for success. That is why The Happy Hustle™ Club was created. This community is here to help 6, 7, & 8+ figure earning entrepreneurs implement The S.O.U.L.M.A.P.P.I.N.™ System. Not just read about it, but be about it. Get bi-weekly Balance Building Trainings, Guest Guru Happy Hours, Happy Hustle Hot Seats, Selfless Service Sessions, and Ca$h Gamified Accountability Challenges while connecting with other world-class Happy Hustlers.

The Ca$h Gamified Accountability is something super unique in that members of The Happy Hustle™ Club can actually win money. Each meeting, members have money at stake as a part of their initial investment into the Club that gets allocated to the monthly antes. If members show up, do what they say they are going to do, and accomplish their SMART goals, they earn their money back and get to split the pot earnings. If they don't complete their stated SMART goals, their money gets forfeited to the pot. Everything is tracked on spreadsheets, and it's a fun way we gamify accountability. If you're interested in joining the Club, apply today at thehappyhustle.com/hub.

◎ ALIGNMENT TAKEAWAY

One of the many lessons I've learned along my journey is that you must pay your dues and develop your skills. As with anything worth doing, it takes time and effort. It takes networking. It takes skill acquisition. It takes Happy Hustlin'. You have to be willing to put forth the energy and spend the hours honing your craft. **Use the 30-30-30 System for Guaranteed Growth every day!** 30 minutes of reading in the morning, 30 minutes of listening in the afternoon, and 30 minutes of watching in the evening, ALL inspirational and educational content related to your goals! Personal Development is key to creating your dream reality, so make sure you are growing and evolving each and every day!

DAILY ACTION TASKS TO HAPPY HUSTLE:

Personal Development

1. Read 30 minutes of an inspirational and educational book.

2. Study, learn, and practice one new skill
that will help you with your work.

3. Reach out to a mentor who is where you want to be
and offer to add value, thus building a relationship.

 # EMBARRASSING FUN FACT

I once snuck into a 3-day long personal development conference.
I didn't have any money at the time and resorted to fabricating
a makeshift badge, dressing in a suit, and waltzing in with
confidence. I sat in the front row soaking up knowledge before
being asked for my credentials and eventually publicly getting
the boot at the end of day 2. #worthit

 # POWERFUL RESOURCES

Books:
The Compound Effect by Darren Hardy
The ONE Thing by Gary Keller
Areté by Brian Johnson

Podcasts:
The School of Greatness with Lewis Howes
Impact Theory with Tom Bilyeu
The Happy Hustle™ Podcast—Episodes #3, #24, #180, & #182

Movie:
The Pursuit of Happyness

HAPPY HUSTLER SPOTLIGHT

Lewis Howes

I started following Lewis Howes online around 2014, before he amassed a successful personal growth business empire. Today, he has touched hundreds of millions of people with his message.

He is a *New York Times* best-selling author, host of a Top 10 globally ranked podcast, entrepreneur, and international motivational speaker. He has connected with the who's who of celebrities because of the platform he created.

He shares his message of *Inspiring Greatness Within* in many formats, including coaching programs, masterminds, training, webinars, books, and podcasts. Back in 2016, I actually got to interview him for a couple of hours at his West Hollywood apartment for a TV show I was hosting. At the time, I had been a part of his School of Greatness Academy and learned a ton from him and his podcast guests. I was very familiar with his message, his humble Ohio roots, and the adversities he faced in his life, like sexual abuse and a devastating, career-ending sports injury. We had a great interview.

One thing that stuck out was how much of a priority he makes personal development and investing in his own growth. He is constantly investing in mentors, coaches, training, and conferences. Success leaves clues,

and Lewis is full of them. Invest in yourself! Lewis never gave up on his dream, and neither should you. He is now changing the lives of millions of people all over the world with his content. He is indeed a Happy Hustler, and one I am grateful to know.

Lewis and me at his place in West Hollywood after crushing an interview. The handlebar mustache was in full effect! Ha!

CHAPTER EIGHT

ALIGNMENT 8: PASSIONATE HOBBIES

Fun is a non-negotiable.

Cary Jack

As I looked out over the vast expanse of Montana's rugged Bob Marshall Wilderness, I couldn't help but feel a sense of awe and excitement. This was the backcountry, and it was here that my dad (a hard-nosed mountain man), my cousin Paul (a loud-mouthed cowpoke from Texas), and a couple of our Montana outdoorsman friends came together for 3 of my favorite hobbies: horseback riding, camping, and fly-fishing. This was set to be a 3-week pack trip expedition that promised awesome adventure.

The mountainous trail crossed rivers, ascended valleys, and traversed cliffs. Towing pack horses loaded with gear, we horseback rode 34 miles for a collective 16 hours in the saddle to get to a fishing utopia very few have been to before. Yes, you read that right; we spent ALL day from before dawn until late into the night riding into this epic spot, all with loudmouth Paul singing songs and bantering about his bravado, sharing what he'd do when/if he saw a bear.

When we finally arrived at the spot, it was well worth the effort we'd made to get there. The scenery was stunning, and the fly-fishing was the best any of us had ever experienced. Every cast resulted in a bite from a beautiful rainbow trout or golden trout, and we celebrated our fishing success by enjoying another one of my hobbies at the time—partying!

Unfortunately, my cousin Paul had more than a few too many, and, not to be gross, but he was throwing up profusely. Because of that, he wasn't allowed in the tent (do you blame us?) and had to sleep outside by the fire. The next morning, he was too hungover to fly-fish with the rest of us, so he stayed lying by the now-smoldering ashes of last night's fire while we made our way down to the river, about 200 yards away from camp.

It wasn't long before we heard a groaning, murmuring sound and just figured it was Paul in his hungover state expressing his agony. But then, we heard his voice yelling, "Buh...buh...BEAR!" My dad and I went running to the campsite, where we found Paul squared up about twenty yards away from a full-sized adult grizzly bear, standing over 10 feet tall, sniffing the air and snorting.

It was a heart-stopping moment for sure! My dad drew his .44 pistol from his hip and fired 2 rounds near the bear to try to scare it away, with no luck. The bear didn't even budge. Our Border Collie was barking like crazy, our horses went running rampant, and our hearts were racing, as we squared up with the king of the wilderness. I had bear pepper spray on me, but I didn't want to discharge it and risk pissing the bear off unless it charged us.

My dad recommended we start throwing rocks at it, a tactic he used in Alaska when encountering grizzly bears. So, after some direct hits (I used to be a pitcher), we annoyed the bear to the point where it finally buggered off and climbed up a tree a ways away. We turned back to Paul, the same guy who had spent 16 hours on our ride into camp boasting about how he would wrestle a bear if we came across one. Instead, he had gotten so scared that he literally soiled himself. Yep, he peed his pants. We all started laughing so hard we were crying, and I still don't let Paul live it down.

Fly-fishing, camping, and horseback riding in the wilderness… they're all still some of my favorite hobbies. As for Paul? He hasn't come back to Montana for a visit since!

HAPPY HUSTLIN' THE FUN STUFF

Alignment 8: Passionate Hobbies is one of my favorite Alignments because it's all about having FUN and relishing the things that light you up outside of work. Yes, I am encouraging you to do things that have no monetary reward; heck, you may even have to pay for them. What is it all for if you're not having fun and enjoying yourself along the journey, right?

I find far too many high-performing entrepreneurs and busy professionals often don't make time for themselves or their hobbies. Most are so focused on their careers, customers, team, spouse, family, kids, etc., and they neglect the person in the mirror. That's a massive mistake.

Engaging in activities you find pleasurable and meaningful can help reduce stress, improve mood, and boost overall well-being. Hobbies can provide a sense of accomplishment and satisfaction, and they can serve as a creative outlet or a means of learning new skills. They can also be a great way to build social networks and connect with others who share your interests. **Engaging in hobbies regularly can help you maintain Happy Hustle harmony and often results in a more fulfilling life experience.**

If you're not rockin' a 5 in this Alignment, it's time to identify what non-work-related activities you love to do and actually *schedule* them into your weekly routine. Whether it's fly-fishing (minus the grizzly bear encounters), oil painting, swing dancing, playing pick-up basketball, playing cards, swimming, or knitting, this is where you give yourself permission to do something that brings you joy and do it regularly!

At a *minimum*, I find spending time on two hobbies per week is the necessary frequency for me to feel balanced, but most weeks it's more than two. Some hobbies I enjoy other than fly-fishing include Krav Maga (Israeli Self-Defense Survival System), playing competitive soccer, and dancing. When I make these hobbies part of my week, I am happier, and my life is more fulfilling because of it.

 PRO TIP: When people ask me which of the martial arts to practice first, I always recommend Krav Maga. It is the most lethal, practical, and efficient of all the many martial arts in which I have trained. It's also my favorite.

The 4 Factors of Fun

When embarking on FUN activities, this is the filter I use to ensure that fun will be had. The given activity must encompass all 4 factors in order to pass, thus earning my time & attention. See, I feel far too many of us get guilted into activities that waste time and energy.

THE 4 FACTORS OF FUN:

1. Does it bring me joy?
2. Will smiling & laughter ensue?
3. Do the others involved raise my vibration?
4. Will I grow?

FUN IS FUNDAMENTAL

My friend, FUN is FUNDAMENTAL. Use the 4 Factors of Fun filter to ensure you're doing things you enjoy regularly, then the trick is to prioritize them with equal importance as work obligations.

PICKIN' PAST & POTENTIAL HOBBIES

If you're not already regularly Happy Hustlin' Passionate Hobbies, let me help get you started. I like to break it down into past & potential hobbies. Past hobbies are those that you have experienced before and have enjoyed. Potential hobbies are those that you have never experienced but may want to. First, we must identify your top 3 favorite past hobbies.

Not sure? Try this:

1. **Make a list:** Start by making a list of all the activities that you have enjoyed doing in your free time. Be as comprehensive as possible, and include anything that comes to mind, from playing sports to creating pottery.

2. **Rank your list:** Once you have a list, rank each activity in order of how much you enjoyed doing it. You might use a scale of 1-10, with 10 being the most enjoyable.

3. **Focus on the top 3:** Look at your ranked list and identify the top 3 activities you enjoy the most. These are likely your top past hobbies.

4. **Schedule them:** Take a moment to reflect on why you enjoyed these top 3 past hobbies. If they still bring you joy at the thought of them, put 'em on the calendar.

5. **Try new things:** Now that we've identified our past hobbies we know bring us joy, we can explore new potential hobbies and add them to the mix. You might discover a new passion or interest that you never knew you had, thus bringing a fresh zest to your life.

HOW TO FIND A NEW POTENTIAL PASSIONATE HOBBY

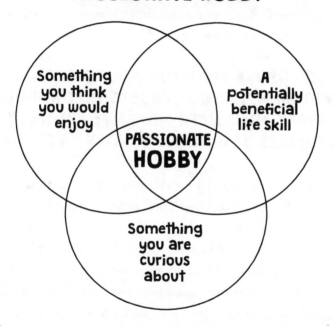

The goal is to have your hobby fit in the center of these 3 qualifying criteria. I recommend identifying at least 3 potential new hobbies you may enjoy. For example, maybe you love music and movement, so learning salsa dancing could be something you think you would enjoy. It is a potentially beneficial life skill for just about any party, as you know that dancing guy or girl draws positive attention while exuding good vibes. And maybe you are curious about the history and culture of the dance. So, voilà, salsa dancing could be a new potential Passionate Hobby!

COMMIT IT TO THE CALENDAR

Once you have decided on your top 3 potential new hobbies, your next step is to actually schedule them. Pick at minimum 1 hobby from each list and schedule them on your calendar for this week. I typically schedule each hobby depending on when it takes place.

For instance, I usually play in a competitive men's soccer league every Sunday morning; Steph and I take dance classes every Wednesday, and Krav Maga is every Tuesday and Thursday evening. Fishing happens whenever I want, either at sunrise or sunset, since that is when the fish are biting best.

TO ENSURE THAT YOU ARE FOLLOWING THROUGH WITH YOUR PASSIONATE HOBBIES, TREAT THEM WITH THE SAME PRIORITY LEVEL AS YOU WOULD A WORK MEETING.

So, choose your activity and then schedule the time at which you will do it. In fact, I suggest you put it in your calendar, then work everything else around it! To ensure that you are following through with your Passionate Hobbies, treat them with the same priority level as you would a work meeting. This means your Zoom business meeting gets the same priority as your pick-up basketball game, and the same goes for your date night with your significant other! All of them get equal priority on your calendar to ensure they get done.

This is a meeting for yourself and must be valued. Without regularly doing these things that you love, your life will become out of balance. Don't let yourself off the hook. It's sometimes easy to cancel on ourselves. Don't do it. Be disciplined enough to prioritize the things that you love to do, not just the things you *have to do*. If you want to be a Happy Hustler, this is an absolute must. Do fun things and enjoy Passionate Hobbies regularly! You earned it!

PRO TIP: If your hobby involves others, you may need to call, text, or email someone to schedule your hobby. Do it. Now! Seriously—stop reading and take action on this. This book was created to actually help you Happy Hustle, not just talk about it. But, you gotta take action. I can show you the door to the blissfully balanced promised land and give you the key. But ultimately, it is you who must open it and go in!

DIVERSIFICATION

Diversification is not only beneficial for your financial investment portfolio, my friend, but it is also beneficial for your hobby portfolio. What are you curious about? What skill or activity have you seen in the movies or online, and thought to yourself, "Dang, I want to try that!" Maybe it's kiteboarding, martial arts, or board games. Who knows what it is for you? The point is to expand yourself and your skill set by doing new things regularly.

Remember that hobbies can change over time, so it's okay to revisit this exercise periodically to see if your top 3 past & potential hobbies have shifted. I am a big advocate for keeping it fresh and not just doing the hobbies you have always done. Consider adding a new one to your life about every 3-6 months.

Keeping your mind open to new potential hobbies means life will never get boring, and you can continue to learn and develop new skills. For instance, I developed an interest in flying planes as a hobby, so I am taking the steps to get my pilot's license and am looking forward to the fun and freedom that comes with piloting my own plane. Plus, developing new skills helps develop neuroplasticity in the brain and actually creates new brain connections. It's not only good for your routine; it's good for your brain to switch it up!

Snowboarding and shreddin' fresh powder on steep mountainous runs are amongst some of my greatest thrills!

Bowhunting for elk in the backcountry wilderness is a Passionate Hobby of mine that combines Optimized Health, Unplugging Digitally, and Nature Connection. That's how you stack Alignments, my friend!

◎ ALIGNMENT TAKEAWAY

Whether you choose to do underwater basket weaving, remote control car racing, or woodworking birdhouses—whatever it is for you, just do it regularly. Feed your soul with fun. Life is too short to postpone your passions. Balance the things you *need* to do with the things you *want* to do. Once again, *balance equals happiness.* **Use the 4 Factors of FUN to determine what past & new potential hobbies to do.** Ask yourself prior to engaging: Does it bring me joy? Will smiling and laughter ensue? Do the others involved raise my vibration? Will I grow? Please, please, please make sure you incorporate Passionate Hobbies into your schedule. Do the things that bring you joy, and do them frequently on your journey of Happy Hustlin' your dream reality!

☑ DAILY ACTION TASKS TO HAPPY HUSTLE:

Passionate Hobbies

1. Schedule 2 Passionate Hobbies on your calendar this week.

2. Research a new potentially interesting hobby to try next quarter.

3. Make a commitment to keep your word to yourself by creating a consequence if you don't do your hobbies. (Consequence Hint: Donating money to a cause you despise always stings.)

😁 EMBARRASSING FUN FACT

Traveling is a hobby I enjoy greatly. In my early 20s (before I was married) while on a trip, I once attempted to join the mile-high club with a beautiful stranger sitting in a neighboring window seat. I boldly wrote on a piece of paper, "You're beautiful. The name's JC. Meet me in the bathroom at 6:30 PM ;)" (JC is/was my alter ego.) I reached over two guys and handed her the paper.

Well, 6:30 PM came around, and guess who came walking down the aisle? The nameless brunette beauty...followed closely by her stern-faced, military-looking general of a father. She walked past with a little smiley smirk and then entered the bathroom. Her father was not so coy as he crouched down 2 inches from my face and said, "You got a lot of f*ing balls, kid. That guy you reached over to hand your forward proposal to was her fiancé. We're on the way to her destination wedding, pal. And the rows around her are full of our family."

My heart sank. He then grabbed me by my thigh with his iron grip and pushed himself up, all the while staring directly into my eyes. He then proceeded back to his seat after his daughter. Talk about an epic failure. Especially since due to bad weather we had to make an emergency landing and de-board then re-board the same plane the next morning. By the end of the flight, not only did all of her family know about the note, but the whole damn plane! That day still goes down in history as one of the most embarrassing moments of my life. The lesson here: traveling is a great hobby. Random mile-high requests, not so much.

🏋️🧠 POWERFUL RESOURCES

Books:
Way of the Peaceful Warrior by Dan Millman (This book changed my life. I even have "Peaceful" & "Warrior" tattooed on my inner biceps. It is 100% worth the read.)
The Alchemist by Paulo Coelho

Podcast:
The Joe Rogan Experience

Online Resource:
OIS Krav Maga with World-Renowned Instructor Philip David Glikman

Television Series:
Primal Survivor with Hazen Audel (friend of mine and awesome Happy Hustler who travels the world showcasing humanity & nature's beauty on epic expeditions)

HAPPY HUSTLER SPOTLIGHT 🔦

Garrett Gravesen

I want to spotlight my Happy Hustlin' friend Garrett Gravesen. He is a world traveler, entrepreneur, author, and storyteller. He definitely knows how to have fun and implement passionate hobbies into his life! Garrett has traveled to all 7 continents and every country in the world. Yes, all 197! That is quite the feat, as less than 300 people out of 7+ billion have done it at the time of this writing! And he's done so wearing a tuxedo to just about all of them.

 I met Garrett at a Brand Builders Group event, and we instantly hit it off. I had him on *The Happy Hustle™ Podcast* Episode #31. Garrett is so charismatic and drops non-stop value bombs in the form of captivating stories. I invite you to listen in; you are gonna love this episode!

He authored the best-selling book *10 Seconds of Insane Courage* (great read). He was recently named one of the "Ten Outstanding Young People of the World." Garrett also co-founded a leadership consulting firm, ADDO Worldwide, and the ADDO Institute.

Garrett is a proud alumnus of Harvard Business School and the University of Georgia, where he was the youngest student body president in school history.

Before attending Harvard, Garrett was an investment banker for Merrill Lynch & Co. in Hong Kong and worked at an AIDS orphanage in Africa for a year. He co-founded H.E.R.O. for Children, the largest pediatric AIDS organization in Georgia, and the Global LEAD Program, which galvanized over 10,000 next-generation leaders' in-service programs in the United

States, Africa, and Europe. He speaks at conferences and companies about innovation, storytelling, and "10 Seconds of Insane Courage." But most of all, he knows how to incorporate his Passionate Hobby of traveling into his life, and we can all learn from that!

This is Garrett in his tux at the bottom of Angel Falls in Venezuela. My man GG is living his best life and Happy Hustlin' around the world.

CHAPTER NINE

ALIGNMENT 9: IMPACTFUL WORK

Your work is going to fill a large part of your life, and the only way to be truly satisfied is to do what you believe is great work. And the only way to do great work is to love what you do.

Steve Jobs

H ere we are, ready to dive into Alignment 9, and I've spent a lot of time up until now sharing with you all the ways I have learned to Happy Hustle and the life-changing joy that comes from it. But what you may not know is that The Happy Hustle™ was actually born from a time in my life when I was absolutely hustlin'... but not happy. In fact, I was miserable. And I want to share it with you as a cautionary tale of what could happen if you don't put the Happy in your Hustle.

Back in 2015, my brother Grant and I were grinding in New York City. We had built a tech startup and designed a software platform called Feedbakr, one that quantified human feedback using an algorithm we created.

Sparing you too many details, our goal was to help people grow by providing them with what they didn't know, essentially giving them feedback after meetings, interviews, and auditions about their performance, directly from the people who were making the decisions through our platform.

Our days consisted of getting up before the sun, throwing on our fancy uncomfortable clothes in an attempt to "dress the tech founders part." Rockin' a $3,000 Prada suit, leopard Tom Ford loafers (both of which I got for pennies on the dollar thanks to a modeling gig), and swanky Persol sunglasses, I headed to the grimy subway with Grant for our 45-minute morning commute, which also included walking blocks in those blister-inducing, flashy, silly shoes.

On a typical day, we'd spend our mornings bustling face-deep in our computers at our entrepreneurial co-working space (an office incubator with other entrepreneurs in downtown Manhattan), then running to a quick lunch meeting. We'd then head back to the office in the afternoon to continue the beta app build-out until it was time for evening cocktails at a networking meet-up. We would attend just about every meet-up and tech community event we could find!

We'd attempt to schmooze somebody important we met by taking them to dinner. Then we'd finish the day with the long subway ride home, and fall into bed just before midnight, only to get up and do it all over again the next day as part of our 100-hour work weeks. At the time, my brother and I were actually sharing a king-sized bed in a dump of an apartment in the Sunnyside Queens neighborhood and ballin' on a budget—to say the least.

We were indeed husltin'. We solicited mentors. We pounded the pavement in search of developers. We cold-called big data partners. We pitched every chance we got, whether in the elevator to a businessman or to a janitor sweeping the floors. We ate, slept, and breathed Feedbakr. With our beta version live and with active users, we were seeking seed investment to build out the full app platform.

Grant and me on the grind at Microsoft offices in NYC

Things really started to roll when we went to a code developers' session at Microsoft that put us in a room we had no business being in. We basically had no clue what they were talking about in the meeting but nodded our heads throughout as if we did. The truth is that we actually were there to poach coders and gain connections. We stayed after that meet-up and discussed the BizSpark program (a Microsoft flagship initiative, which was set up to provide technology, support, visibility, and an interactive community experience to promising startups and entrepreneurs) with the Microsoft liaison. It was a very informative meeting, and we left with a plan of attack to apply.

The next day we went to a talk at Spotify with a panel of distinguished tech evangelists. One of the panelists was an executive at IBM, so of course we pitched him on our business, and he seemed interested. He actually set us up a meeting at IBM with his whole team later that week to hear more. At the time, IBM offered a Global Entrepreneurship Program (their version to rival Microsoft's BizSpark program), which parleyed into seed investment, cloud storage, and tech support. This was a massive meeting for us.

With admission to this program, everything could change, and we knew it. In the days leading up to the meeting, we studied and researched nearly everything ever published about IBM. We put in the time and energy to become fully prepared.

When it came time to execute, we were confident and collected, but to be completely transparent, we were also a little intimidated walking into the 100-something-floor high-rise conference room in downtown Manhattan, complete with a mahogany table and a collection of IBM executives, all in full business mode.

We marched into the meeting wearing our finest (tech-founder-esque) suits, slide deck ready, printouts with our financial projections and business plan summarized in hand, ready to crush it. But the meeting didn't go as planned...

We anticipated the IBM executives would grill us on our business, but what happened was actually the reverse. We led with the fact that we were at Microsoft earlier in the week discussing the

BizSpark program (essentially their biggest competitor). Of course, we left out that we had only dropped in on a meet-up and didn't actually have a legit offer to join!

With this status shift, the dynamic changed, and *we* ended up asking *them* the questions: *Why do you think we should join your program? How can IBM best serve us?* They pitched us so hard! It was actually quite hilarious in hindsight, almost a cliché compound by-product of "fake it 'til you make it" mixed with "knowledge is power." We left that meeting not only with an offer to join the program, but also with a massive funding offer to follow shortly!

But ultimately, we were hesitant when it came down to accepting the 7-figure VC funding deal that came with a 5-year commitment clause (rightfully so, if someone's going to give you that much money, they want to make sure you're in it to win it). Regardless, we just knew deep down in our souls we couldn't take the money, even though it would have most definitely been the catalyst for our startup company becoming a viable mainstream business making potentially big-time money with a massive future exit.

We knew that taking the deal would be like getting stuck in quicksand. We would be trapped for at least the next 5 years in the business, slowly sinking into unsatisfying sorrow, unsustainable routines, and ultimately massive unfulfillment.

WE WERE BOTH EXHAUSTED AND COMPLETELY BURNED OUT.

So, before finalizing the funding deal and inking the paperwork to solidify the offer and partnerships, Grant and I had a heart-to-heart conversation. We were both exhausted and completely burned out. We weren't taking care of our health, our relationships with family and friends were virtually non-existent, and all we were doing was working. Tears streamed from our eyes as we sat across from one another at the watermark-stained table in the scrap yard of a kitchen we called home.

After we acknowledged that we were feeling unhappy and unfulfilled, it was time to get crystal clear on what my brother and I really wanted. What was our true vision for our lives? What did we wish to create? What was God's plan for us? We wanted to make a positive impact on the planet, but we understood deep down that it was going to have to happen in a different form. In that moment, we decided it was best for us and the business to make a tremendous shift.

We made an extremely difficult decision to fold the business, say no to the funding deal and partnerships, and move on in a different direction. My brother and I left New York and went our separate ways, with him searching for meaning and purpose in the form of a master's degree at the University of Florida, and me traveling overseas to live in Bangkok, Thailand for 10+ months.

It was in Thailand that I realized there was a better way to work and live. A way to actually enjoy the journey while infusing meaning into my work. A way to put the Happy in my everyday Hustle. A way to make income and impact by doing something I truly enjoyed! And so, The Happy Hustle™ was born. My goal in sharing this story is to show you that even if you happen to be hustlin' for the wrong reasons currently, or are misaligned with unfulfilling work, it is not too late to make a change and create purposeful, Impactful Work, my friend.

THE PROBLEM WITH IMPACTFUL WORK

The first step in creating a purposeful business or career is acknowledging your current reality. Think about where you ranked yourself in this Impactful Work Alignment (1-5). Are you working a job you dislike or even hate? Do you wake up and dread what you do in exchange for money? Is there conflict with your boss or co-workers? You must truly identify where you currently are in terms of your Impactful Work or lack thereof.

Furthermore, if you are a leader of a team, know that well-being affects employee engagement and performance. As Gallup states, "Engaged employees produce far better outcomes, but Gallup recently discovered that engaged workers who are not thriving in their lives are much more vulnerable and add risk to your organization. Comparing employees who are engaged but not thriving with those who are engaged and thriving, those who aren't thriving report the following risks:

- 61% more likely to experience burnout often or always
- 48% more likely to report daily stress
- 66% more likely to experience daily worry
- 2x more likely to report daily sadness and anger" [1]

Again, referring back to Gallop's *State of The Global Workplace* research study, 3 out of every 4 employees are disengaged and unhappy with their work. So if you lead a team or personally fall in that category, know that you are not alone and there's a way to fix it!

I recommend making a game plan for how you are going to improve your current career or company if it is not fulfilling. You have the power to change your reality. You have the ability to be brave and make a different choice. It's time to say no to what you don't want and *hell yes* to what you do. You can Happy Hustle a new & improved future with purposeful, Impactful Work, and it starts right now.

7 CATALYSTS TO BOOST EMPLOYEE WELL-BEING

If you are a leader or business owner, this is for you. And it's important because happy employees are reported to be more productive. Gallup identified 7 Catalysts that employers can use to support and change their employees' well-being. Each of the 7 Catalysts can be used to address and better support employees across the 5 elements of well-being, which are: physical, financial, community, career, and social well-being. So these 7 Catalysts can help you and your team Happy Hustle a more productive, engaged, and joyful culture.

The 7 Catalysts are:

- **Development:** Do your development plans include well-being goals?

- **Recognition:** Do you share and celebrate well-being successes?

- **Communication:** Are your messages, especially from leaders and managers, consistent with a high-performing and net-thriving culture?

- **Incentives:** Do they inspire participation in activities that produce results?

- **Events:** Do they build awareness of net-thriving culture and change behaviors?

- **Rules & Guidelines:** Do they work for or against thriving in each of the 5 elements?

- **Facilities:** Is it easy to move around your office space, see outdoors, and collaborate?

I hope you leverage these 7 Catalysts to increase your employees' well-being and help them put the Happy in their Hustle. As leaders, we must take responsibility not only for our own well-being but for our teams as well.

As John Clifton says,

The real fix is this simple: better leaders in the workplace. Managers need to be better listeners, coaches, and collaborators. Great managers help colleagues learn and grow, recognize their colleagues for doing great work, and make them truly feel cared about. In environments like this, workers thrive. Business units with engaged workers have 23% higher profit compared with business units with miserable workers. Additionally, teams with thriving workers see significantly lower absenteeism, turnover, and accidents; they also see higher customer loyalty. The point is, well-being at work isn't at odds with anyone's agenda.[2]

This section alone could be the intel needed to shift and create a massive ripple effect of Impactful Work in your company, so I hope it resonates. If you lead a team, I believe it is your responsibility to help your team put the Happy in their Hustle!

3 QUESTIONS TO IMPACTFUL WORK

Let's say hypothetically right now you are not running a company, but rather you are working in a career that you would not deem Impactful Work. I want to share with you how you can align yourself with your true calling. And if you are leading a team or own a company, you can use this process to connect more deeply with your people. As my friends at Brand Builders Group teach as a part of their curriculum, start by asking yourself these 3 questions:

1. WHAT problem do you feel called to solve?

2. WHO do you feel called to solve that problem for?

3. What is your UNIQUENESS in solving the problem, and how can you exploit it in the service of others?

And I'll add one more bonus of my own:

4. What is your HAPPY HUSTLIN' WHY?

 PRO TIP: Your Happy Hustlin' Why should be deeper than just making money. It should be something that will truly be the fuel to your fire, helping you push past the inevitable adversity along the journey. Plus, If you're interested in going deeper on these questions, check out brandbuildersgroup.com to build, grow, and monetize your personal brand!

The WHAT

"Business is all about solving people's problems at a profit," as my friend & successful entrepreneur Wade T. Lightheart says. He is the co-founder of the multi-million-dollar company BIOptimizers. (Check out episode #109 on *The Happy Hustle™ Podcast* to listen to the awesome interview I did with him.)

THE ONE-WORD PROBLEM THAT I SOLVE IS IMBALANCE. IT'S WHY I WROTE THIS BOOK, TO HELP YOU AVOID BURNOUT AND ACHIEVE BLISSFUL BALANCE BOTH PERSONALLY AND PROFESSIONALLY.

Don't overcomplicate it. Just think, what problem do you actually want to solve? What cause speaks to you personally? How could you combine your skills and knowledge to create a solution?

Do your best to distill the problem that you solve into ONE word. That type of specificity will ensure the clarity necessary for success. For me, the one-word problem that I solve is *imbalance*. It's why I wrote this book, to help you avoid burnout and achieve Blissful Balance both personally and professionally. To help you systematically harmonize ambition & well-being, aka Happy Hustle! Think about what that one word could be for you.

If you're stuck here, ponder what you have overcome that gives you the right to solve that same problem for others. Most often our mess becomes our message, so think about what that is for you. Decide what problem that is and how you can be the one to solve it with a product or service. In one word—clarity!

The WHO

Now that you have the WHAT, the WHO is imperative. If you solve problems for people that you don't like to be around, then you will find yourself dreading the act of helping them. Choose to solve the problem for a targeted niche of the population who you actually want to serve and associate yourself with. Personally, I love solving the problem of imbalance for purpose-driven entrepreneurs like me. I feel happiest helping other heart-centered high-performers on a similar mission to spread their message. Oftentimes, we like solving problems for those who are in our old shoes or who are where we have been in the past.

Once you can identify the target niche you want to solve the problem for, go a mile deep and an inch wide. Most companies and entrepreneurs say, "I can help everyone!" They go a mile wide and an inch deep, then wonder why their marketing doesn't land. Happy Hustlers instead spend the time to find out everything about their perfect target avatar by going a mile deep.

Sure, they delve into demographics like age, sex, location, marital status, income, etc. But more importantly, they ascertain psychographics, like personality traits, lifestyle choices, opinions, beliefs, morals, interests, etc. When you can get to know your perfect target avatar at this level of detail, you can cut through the noisy marketplace and speak directly to their soul with your message.

With this clarity, instead of *pushing* marketing content, you will be *pulling* opportunity seekers into your world. **Instead of being a megaphone, you can rather be a magnet, magnetizing your perfect people as customers.** Once you have your perfect avatar's attention, you can add value to them and nurture a relationship. The key point here is to actually *nurture* the relationship. Don't just go right for the sale before adding sufficient value and building trust (refer back to the R.O.A.D.M.A.P. $ales $ystem in Alignment 6 Abundance Financially). When the time is right, you can present them with your product or service to solve their problem. Voilà! You're making money solving a problem you care about for people you care about, thus creating Impactful Work and fulfillment.

The UNIQUENESS

Now, the next level to crushing purposeful, Impactful Work is exploiting your uniqueness in the service of others. You may be thinking, "But Cary, I don't know what the heck my uniqueness is!"

Here's a quick way to figure it out. Ask your 10 closest relationships in your life what attribute of yours they appreciate the most, then write down each response, and note the most common, similar answers.

If you don't want to reach out to others in your inner circle, then write down 5 things that make you feel authentically you, and 5 things you feel you are uniquely good at. Look at both lists and pick the top one from each list to combine into a uniqueness you can bring to serve your perfect avatar. If you feel your uniqueness is unclear, then you may need to acquire new skills to add to your repertoire in order to make yourself unique.

Your HAPPY HUSTLIN' WHY

Although many use and define the word differently, when I have been discussing Hustlin' in this book, I mean doing whatever it takes to get what you want—staying up late, waking up early, making cold calls, showing up without a meeting, getting rejected over and over again, but still continuing anyway. Hustlin' usually only occurs when you want something bad enough that you're willing to do whatever it takes to get it. When you are prepared to put in the sweat equity. When time spent doesn't matter, only getting results does.

> ## TO HUSTLE HARDER THAN EVER BEFORE, YOU HAVE TO FIND YOUR WHY DEEP WITHIN YOURSELF.

To hustle harder than ever before, you have to find your *why* deep within yourself. What is the purpose behind your efforts? Why are you doing it? Why do you want what you want? This is your fuel. When you are feeling down, rejected, or discouraged, the *why* is what will lift you up to keep pushing. The thoughts of status and material things typically aren't strong enough for you to persevere in the toughest of times. Your *why* needs to be emotionally charged.

My *why* for the longest time stemmed from my mom being sick most of my life. Due to her illness, my family moved 24 times before

I was 18 years old. I watched her suffer for years while struggling with her health. I want so badly to build her a healthy, toxin-free home, supply her with top-notch support (supplements, equipment, testing, etc.), and provide her with the world's best professional care to heal. It fuels me every day. The pain from her experience (along with my own relentless drive) pushes me to do whatever it takes. When you find a reason worth pursuing, it will change everything. Your *why* may change over time, and that's ok.

I recently became a father to a beautiful son, which has become a whole new *why*. I truly have not felt urgency like this before and am on fire to get things accomplished to be the best father, husband, provider, and protector for my family. So whatever it is for you, just make sure to have a *why* so strong it fuels you past the inevitable adversity.

THE HAPPY HUSTLE-DOTE FORMULA

I created a proven and tested formula for Hustlin' that I use every day. So once you have your What, Who, Uniqueness, and Why clear... this is how to actually put Happy Hustlin' into practice for Impactful Work.

THE HAPPY HUSTLE–DOTE FORMULA

PREPARATION

Means doing the research ahead of time. Knowing the details of the objective. Outlining a plan.

+

EXECUTION

Is following through on that plan. Utilizing all information and necessary means. Doing whatever it takes.

=

HUSTLE–DOTE

Is the remedy to achieve the result. The actions necessary to accomplish The Happy Hustler's formula.

TIME

Our most precious commodity. With the time ticking away, how quickly can you implement and achieve?

+

ENERGY

Is an asset we possess but must use wisely. How intelligently we utilize energy in pursuit of the result will dictate the outcome.

HUSTLE–DOTE

Is the remedy to achieve the result. The actions necessary to accomplish The Happy Hustler's formula.

X

PERSISTENT CONSISTENCY

Means every day getting closer through smart action. Putting in the work. Doing the little things consistently.

=

RESULTS

Are whatever you want or desire. The tangible or intangible outcome. The consequence of your actions.

- **Preparation** means doing the research ahead of time. Knowing the details of the objective. Outlining a plan.

- **Execution** is following through on that plan, using all of the information and any necessary means. Doing whatever it takes.

- **Time** is our most precious commodity. With the time ticking away, how quickly can you implement and achieve your plan?

- **Energy** is an asset we possess but must use wisely. How intelligently we spend our focused energy in pursuit of the result will dictate the outcome.

- **Happy Hustle-Dote** is the process to achieve the plan. These components are essential to accomplish. This is the Happy Hustler's formula for success.

- **Persistent Consistency** means every day getting closer through smart action. Putting in the work. Doing the little things consistently.

- **Results** are whatever you want or desire. The tangible or intangible outcome of the plan followed. The consequence of your actions.

You can use the Happy Hustle-Dote to achieve everything you want in life and more. Used in conjunction with a clear vision, it will yield the desired results in your life. Don't take this lightly. This is the golden ticket to your chocolate factory, boys and girls. If you've got a sweet tooth for a sweet life, use the Happy Hustle-Dote to satisfy that craving and Happy Hustle your dream reality!

MONEY & HAPPINESS

Now, you may be saying, This all sounds great, but I need to make money! Agreed—we all do. Money is a tool, a form of stored energy. And it is indeed essential to Happy Hustle a life you love.

However, most people don't truly assess how much they *actually* need to be happy. Nobel Prize-winning economist Angus Deaton found that after an individual in the United States earns $75,000 a year, the direct correlation between money and happiness dissipates. Essentially, that means once you have your basic needs met,[3] money isn't directly associated with your overall happiness.

Now, given inflation, the devaluation of our currency, and other factors, I believe that number is higher and will continue to rise each year. Regardless, the point is most of us need a lot less than we think we do to be happy. You must get clear on your actual Happiness Income annual number, which is going to differ based on your individual situation and variables such as if you are married, have kids, where you live, your desired lifestyle, etc.

If you don't get clear on your Happiness Income annual number, you will spend your life always seeking more and never really being content. So decide now what is that number for you? $250K a year after taxes? $500K? $1 million? $10 million? Then reverse engineer how to get there! Remember, you can be Happy within the Hustle even if you don't earn your Happiness Income annual number currently.

THE "MORE DISEASE"

I call it the "more disease," and chances are, you might have already been infected by it. But don't worry—I've got the cure!

We all desire more in life—more money, more impact, more clients, more followers, more success, more love, and so on! It's human nature to always want more. However, this insatiable desire can become a disease that robs us of joy, happiness, abundance, and fulfillment. The pursuit of more can leave us feeling empty and dissatisfied.

One of the significant contributors to the "more disease" is the tendency to compare ourselves to others. Social media platforms often serve as a breeding ground for comparison, as we are constantly exposed to curated highlight reels of other people's lives. Instead, I suggest you compare yourself to who you were yesterday and strive to get better every day.

But here's the secret ingredient to cure yourself of the "more disease," and that is gratitude. Finding gratitude for exactly where you are right now, even if it's not where you want to be, is the key to increasing your happiness. You can find gratitude by measuring yourself backward against where you started and how far you've come. Dan Sullivan, founder of Strategic Coach, says that if you measure yourself against where you started and find gratitude for your present, you can find joy; if you measure yourself against your ideal horizon, which is an ever-changing goal post, you often will find unfulfillment.

It is a powerful tool in combating "more disease." When we practice gratitude, we shift our focus from what we lack to what we already have. It's easy to get caught up in a never-ending cycle of wanting more possessions, more achievements, and more recognition.

It can be as simple as taking a few minutes each day to reflect on the things we are grateful for. It could be as basic as having a roof over our heads, food on the table, or the support of loved ones. By consciously directing our attention to the positives, we reframe our mindset and begin to recognize the abundance that surrounds us.

So, my friend, it's time to say goodbye to the "more disease" and put the Happy back into your everyday Hustle. Embrace the power of gratitude, be persistently consistent in your pursuits, and compare yourself to who you were yesterday. Focus on incremental improvements and celebrate your progress along the way!

◎ ALIGNMENT TAKEAWAY

So, there you have it. 7 Catalysts to boost employee well-being, 3 questions (plus a bonus) for you to align yourself with your calling, and the Happy Hustle-Dote to help you achieve Impactful Work in your life today!

If you already have a thriving, happy team, use the 7 Catalysts to enhance what you're already doing. If you already feel purpose and impact in your work, amazing! Use these questions to dive deeper and become even more clear so you can help even more people: your team, your family, and your friends. The world needs your message. Take action. Don't sacrifice your time doing meaningless work or being unfulfilled any longer. The time is now for you to combine your passion and purpose into Impactful Work that actually makes a positive difference in the world.

We are all on a mission for meaning. Don't waste another moment sacrificing your soul doing work you despise. Answer your calling. Create the Impactful Work in your life that you crave. You can make money doing something you enjoy. But you must earn that right by *doing the work*. Answer the 4 questions to Impactful Work. Get crystal clear on your vision and make a plan. Then use the **Happy Hustle-Dote** to achieve it! You got this baby!

> ## WE ARE ALL ON A MISSION FOR MEANING. DON'T WASTE ANOTHER MOMENT SACRIFICING YOUR SOUL DOING WORK YOU DESPISE.

 ## DAILY ACTION TASKS TO HAPPY HUSTLE:

Impactful Work

1. Journal the Happy Hustle-Dote with specificity for your goals and the next steps to accomplish today.

2. Share a post on social media giving value via your uniqueness.

3. Reach out to 1 individual today who has the Impactful Work you seek in your industry and offer to creatively support them.

☺ EMBARRASSING FUN FACT

One of The Happy Hustle™ tactics I have used regularly throughout my journey up the ranks is exploiting free trials and the system behind them. If you are not aware, many businesses and companies give out free trials. Take, for example, WeWork.

WeWork is an amazing collaborative workspace for hip, outgoing entrepreneurs and business people. At the time of this writing, WeWork offers free tours & trial days at all of their buildings. They have facilities all over the world in nearly every major city. While my brother and I were getting our hustle on during the growth stages of our first 3 startups, we used to find free office space all over the cities we were in (especially when were in NYC). The best part was the network effect. Instead of having the boring, awkward watercooler talk, we would make a point to engage with as many co-workers as possible with probing questions, then listen and learn.

These incubators and collaborative offices usually attract some cool companies with innovative entrepreneurs, and we created the opportunity to rub elbows with as many as possible. We would go to incubators, like WeWork, do a tour of the facility, act very interested in signing up for membership/office space, and then request a trial day. We often would plan our tours around the incubator event schedules so we could get some work in and then get our networking on. Usually the events are catered with food and drinks, so yeah, we got more than a few free meals this way.

Even when we were just visiting cities, many times instead of working out of an often distracting, busy coffee shop, we would find incubators, request a tour, and then a trial work day, failing to mention our transient status. We have probably repeated this process in at least a dozen different cities at a ton of incubator workspaces. We would even schedule full-on meetings with potential partners/clients/employees at the incubators that we had never been to yet. So a bit embarrassing, sure, but that's how we would exploit the "free-trial system" for office spaces in particular. And, for the record, I have since paid for a full-on WeWork membership.

 PRO TIP: Many businesses will offer free trials to courses, software, etc., and some may not even have a formal free-trial policy in place, but will still give you one, so you just have to ask. *A Happy Hustler always asks.* A Happy Hustler always finds a way!

POWERFUL RESOURCES

Books:
DotCom Secrets by Russell Brunson
Extreme Ownership by Jocko Willink & Leif Babin
The Common Path to Uncommon Success by John Lee Dumas

Podcasts:
The Influential Personal Brand Podcast with Rory & AJ Vaden
Impact Theory with Tom Bilyeu
The Ed Mylett Show with Ed Mylett
Entrepreneurs on Fire with John Lee Dumas

Movie:
Steve Jobs

HAPPY HUSTLER SPOTLIGHT 🔦

John Lee Dumas

John Lee Dumas is an Army veteran, founder of Podcasters' Paradise, and host of the award-winning podcast *Entrepreneurs on Fire*. With over 150 million listens of his 5000+ episodes, JLD has turned *Entrepreneurs on Fire* into a media empire that generates over a million listens every month and 7 figures of net annual revenue 10+ years in a row.

His first traditionally published book, *The Common Path to Uncommon Success*, is the modern-day version of *Think and Grow Rich* with a revolutionary 17-step roadmap to financial freedom and fulfillment.

JLD is for sure a Happy Hustler, living in a beautiful beach home in Puerto Rico (which saves him millions in taxes). JLD interviews with so much spunky energy, and he knows how to extract usable value

JLD and me after the float tanks

that actually teaches his audience. A true pioneer in the industry, he even started out by releasing daily podcast episodes, something no one else was doing at the time.

JLD leverages systems and discipline to accomplish anything he sets his mind to. He has created purposeful work that truly impacts millions of entrepreneurs' lives all over the world. His content, courses, books, videos, podcasts, and messages inspire and educate, and he is an example of what is possible when you stay consistent and committed. He is a Happy Hustler through and through. I had the chance to personally connect with JLD, and we have since built an amazing friendship. He even gave me a testimonial quote for this very book (check out the back cover). He even came out for one of our recent Montana Mastermind Epic Camping Adventures, and we had a blast together mixing business with pleasure in the beautiful backcountry wilderness. I am grateful for him and the positive impact he has had on my entrepreneurial journey. Check out more about him and his award-winning podcast (listen to the multiple episodes I was featured on by typing Cary Jack in the search) at eofire.com.

JLD!

JLD came out to the July 2023 Montana Mastermind Epic Camping Adventure along with other badass high-performing entrepreneurs, and we had a blast mixing business with pleasure in the backcountry wilderness!

CHAPTER TEN

ALIGNMENT 10: NATURE CONNECTION

*How you climb a mountain is more
important than reaching the top.*

Yvon Chouinard

Surfing is another activity I enjoy but admittedly am not very good at. However, it's a way I can Happy Hustle two Alignments at once: Passionate Hobbies (Alignment 8) and Nature Connection (Alignment 10).

When you think of Nature Connection, maybe you think of a pleasant stroll through the park or a picnic by a lake. And those would be great, for sure! But at this point in the book, I think you know me well enough to guess that my Nature Connection sometimes (ok, often!) includes at least a little bit of a nail-biting death-defying outdoor adventure!

And that was the case on a beautiful evening in Northern California. I was with my buddy at Steamer Lane in Santa Cruz, a famous surf site due to its world-class waves and jagged rocky point (great for spectators wanting to watch) that attract surfers from all over the globe. The point break at Steamer Lane produces consistent waves that are fast, steep, and challenging, making it a prime location for experienced surfers seeking a thrilling ride. (It's probably worth noting here again that while I enjoy surfing, it would be a stretch to call me "experienced" by Steamer Lane standards.) The waves are shaped by unique underwater rock formations and strong currents, resulting in a dynamic surfing environment that tests the skills of even the most skilled surfers.

Despite my lack of experience, I felt the urge to jump off The Point, a rocky outcrop that juts out into the ocean and creates a distinctive and challenging surf break. Here you'll find powerful waves that can reach heights of up to 20 feet. Even though it was dusk and my body was still digesting a big late-afternoon meal, I jumped off. It wasn't long at all before I felt a sudden immense cramp on the entire left side of my body, leaving me with only one good arm and a partially functioning right leg.

I was alone, hundreds of yards away from shore, and getting swept by the current. Just when I thought things couldn't get any worse, something bumped my board, and I was 100% convinced that a shark was coming after me. With my heart pounding even harder, I turned to see that it was just a seal swimming by, but that wasn't great news either—as seals are bait for the Great Whites in the area! Fortunately, a pod of dolphins showed up next. I took this as a good sign, because it's generally accepted that sharks aren't in the immediate area if dolphins are there. I was basically frozen in the midst of this real-time Animal Planet oceanic episode.

A pic from that fateful day at Steamer Lane in Santa Cruz, CA before I almost died. Yes, the water was freezing cold and full-body wetsuits were necessary!

As I struggled to figure out how to get back to shore with the sun setting rapidly, I caught sight of my friend off in the foggy distance, so I paddled with one arm to get closer to him. When I got within shouting distance, I hollered, "Hey, man, I need some help!"

Once he understood my problem, he shouted back to me, "All right, I'm going to point out the smallest wave that you should take, and just body surf it in!"

In just a matter of minutes, as I got myself into position, I thought I heard him yelling, "Go! Go! Go!" as the next set rolled in. Except that's not what he was *actually* yelling. What he saw was a giant swell coming at me, so he was shouting, "NO! NO! NO!"

I started paddling with my one good arm, attempting to body surf the wave in. I got picked up by the wave and folded like a lawn chair deep down into the ocean abyss. I was pummeled by the ocean's power. I fought for air as I was hit by one wave after another after another, not knowing which way was up, out of breath, drowning, and feeling like I was literally about to die.

Suddenly a hand reached under the water where I was tumbling, grabbed the back of my wetsuit, and pulled me up onto a longboard. It was an older, veteran surfer who may as well have been an angel. "DUDE!" he scolded me. "You have no business being out here!"

"Yeah, I know that now!" I answered exhaustedly.

After that memorable experience, I respect the power of nature more than ever. It's something we all have to respect and protect. Nature can be unpredictable, yes, but it's also essential to our well-being. And connecting with nature is a non-negotiable for Happy Hustlers.

GET OUTSIDE!

The unfortunate reality is that many of us get so caught up in our job and other obligations that we routinely forget to stop and smell (or even notice) the flowers, trees, or nature around us. It's like we're tunnel-visioned and completely lacking our primal spirit of connection to Pachamama ("Earth Mother" in Inca mythology).

Where did you rank yourself in Alignment 10: Nature Connection (1-5)? If you're low in this Alignment, let's prioritize change accordingly. In order to be more balanced and connected with nature…you have to *actually* leave your house and *actually* get outside! I know—crazy, right?

> **I ASK, DO YOU WANT TO INCREASE YOUR HAPPINESS? THEN GET OUTSIDE MORE AND TUNE INTO NATURE!**

Seriously, though. Most of us are living like zoo animals. We're caged in our homes and apartments, and if we don't do our work from that cage, we transition to our cage on wheels to then arrive at our office cage, which may not even have a view!

If we're lucky, at some point in the day we may get in a quick run outside or a walk in the park, but most of us are more likely to exercise in the indoor gym cage, all the while soaking up toxic blue lights and recycled air. According to The National Human Activity Pattern Survey (NHAPS)[1], roughly 90% of people's time is spent indoors! That's a crazy but all-too-true statistic.

So, I ask, *do you want to increase your happiness?* Then get outside more and tune into nature!

Not only will getting outside provide physical benefits, such as improving cardiovascular health and increasing vitamin D levels, but it can also have positive effects on mental well-being by reducing stress levels. Get barefoot and walk on the grass. Take a dip in a natural body of water (not a pool with chemicals). Exercise by going on a hike in a park instead of doing the elliptical at the gym. Make it a priority to spend time outside and connect with the beauty and wonder of the natural world.

THE 3-DAY EFFECT

There's nothing like the great outdoors. We humans have been living in and enjoying the great outdoors for hundreds of thousands of years. It was only within the last 100 years have we really started to live indoors. And in the last 50 years, we have been inundated with technology in our everyday reality.

Most of us have lost touch with nature and have been disconnected from our beautiful planet's amazing natural environment and its benefits. Well, new studies show the benefits of being outdoors for 3 days.

David Sawyer, a cognitive psychologist at the University of Utah, coined the term The 3-Day Effect. Those in nature for 3 days showed lower prefrontal cortex activity, a brain region that, when overstimulated, is responsible for stress, depression, and anxiety.

Other documented benefits from exposure to 3 days in nature include:

- Lower Blood Pressure
- Improved Memory
- Elevated Mood
- Better Sleep Quality
- Increased Self-Esteem
- Better Vitamin Absorption
- Stronger Immune System

So exposing yourself to nature has been scientifically shown to improve both mental and physical health. Research has shown that nature sounds or even outdoor silence can lower cortisol, the stress hormone that activates our fight-or-flight response.

A nature setting may also correlate to a likelier receptiveness to introspection, positive internal dialogue, and overall increased happiness. That's why the Montana Mastermind Epic Camping Adventure exists and why it is the duration it is… more on that later.

PROTECT OUR PLANET

As our society continues to advance, we are unfortunately sacrificing more natural land to make room for commercial and residential development. While I'm not opposed to progress, I strongly believe that we must find a way to restore the critical balance between humanity and the natural world. In fact, I feel that this is one of the primary purposes for my existence—to help raise awareness and restore harmony between people and our planet.

> **IF WE DON'T TAKE ACTION TO PROTECT OUR ENVIRONMENT, WE WILL SOON FIND THAT THERE ISN'T MUCH NATURE LEFT FOR US TO ENJOY.**

If we don't take action to protect our environment, we will soon find that there isn't much nature left for us to enjoy. We are currently destroying our natural resources and ecosystems at an alarming pace, with devastating consequences. We are drilling in untouched wilderness for fossil fuels, cutting down majestic forests for paper products and timber, and mining the earth for coal, plutonium, and other natural elements. We are even extracting our natural spring water and bottling it in toxic plastic containers.

These unsustainable practices are having a profound impact on the health of our planet, and we have to change our ways, *now.* We need to work towards implementing regenerative, eco-friendly practices that are truly sustainable. Our food sources are often genetically modified and contaminated with dangerous pesticides, tainting our soil, and this is just the tip of the iceberg. (Watch the movie *Kiss the Ground* if you haven't already.) We are living unsustainably, and it is time for us to make a change.

We must act now to protect our environment and honor Pachamama, not just for ourselves, but for future generations and the other animal species that called this place home. It is critical that we make a massive shift in the next decade, or we risk irreversible damage.

BE A PART OF THE SOLUTION, NOT THE PROBLEM.

Now I didn't mean to get all doom and gloom on ya there, but it is the truth. Major corporations in big industries such as oil, gas, logging, agriculture, power, mining, telecommunications, plastic, and pharma are exploiting Planet Earth for their personal gain with little remorse and virtually no regulation. If we want to stop them before it is too late, we need to come together and speak up! So take stock of your and your company's footprint, and be accountable. Be a part of the solution, not the problem.

BE AN ECO—WARRIOR

I strongly encourage you to Happy Hustle your way to becoming an eco-warrior and advocating for the good of the planet. There are many eco-causes you can volunteer for to help protect the environment and promote sustainability. Here are a few examples:

- **Conservation efforts:** You can volunteer with organizations that work to protect and restore natural habitats and ecosystems. This can involve activities such as planting trees, removing invasive species, and monitoring wildlife populations.

- **Cleanups:** You can participate in beach, river, or park cleanups to remove litter and debris from natural areas. This can help to prevent pollution and protect wildlife from harm. Check out my bro Alex's company 4ocean for ocean cleanups!

- **Sustainable agriculture:** You can volunteer with organizations that promote sustainable farming practices, such as reducing pesticide use, promoting crop rotation, and increasing biodiversity. This can help to improve the health of the soil and reduce the environmental impact of agriculture.

- **Climate action:** You can volunteer with organizations that work to address climate change, such as promoting renewable energy, reducing carbon emissions, and advocating for policy changes that support sustainability.

- **Environmental education:** You can volunteer with organizations that promote environmental education and awareness, such as leading nature walks, teaching sustainable living practices, and organizing educational events and workshops.

Those are just a few examples of eco-causes people can volunteer for. But there are also many other small ways you can take a stand, get involved, and make a difference for the environment:

- Be a conscious consumer. Vote every day with your dollar. Only support ethical businesses that focus on the Triple Bottom Line—People, Planet, and Profits. They are out there. Don't support companies that participate in unsustainable business practices.

- Look specifically to support B-Corporations. It may be a little less convenient than buying on Amazon, but spend the extra 5 minutes online properly researching and vetting the companies you buy from. It may even cost you a couple of extra bucks to purchase eco-friendly dish soap or laundry detergent, but I promise you, collectively it will make a difference.

- Bring your own reusable bags to the grocery. Use a reusable water bottle. Bring your own reusable straws & cutlery.

- Be conscious of your water and electricity usage.

- Buy local fruits, veggies, and meat to support your farmers.

- When it comes to unsustainable products and materials like plastic: Refuse, Reduce, Reuse, and Recycle (yes, in that order).

- Eat less factory-farmed meats and vegetables.

Be an eco-warrior every day by making conscious choices. The little daily decisions have a compound effect, as my man Darren Hardy says, so be deliberate with your everyday choices. You can make a difference!

 PRO TIP: If you want to learn more about becoming an eco-warrior and what my brother and I are doing, and how you can get involved, check out our company EcoBreakthroughs.com!

TRIPLE BOTTOM LINE—PEOPLE, PLANET, AND PROFITS

If you are serious about being a Happy Hustler, then the Triple Bottom Line needs to be a priority. Focusing on 3 key areas as a business leader is how to ensure the health of our planet, happiness, and our bank accounts. Use the Triple Bottom Line and keep the 3 P's top of mind—People, Planet, and Profits—while you Happy Hustle your dream reality!

THE TRIPLE BOTTOM LINE

1. People
2. Planet
3. Profits

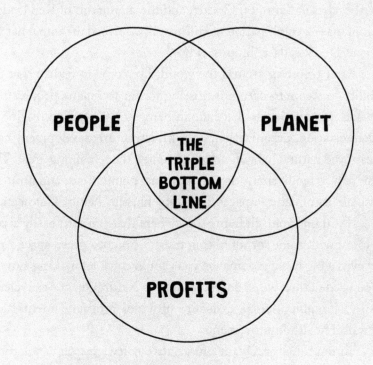

TIME TO MOVE?

I've lived all over the world, from Bangkok to Barcelona, Rio de Janeiro to Buenos Aires, Miami to LA, but one place still and always has had my heart—Montana, with its abundance of untouched natural beauty.

Years ago, my wife and I moved to Montana primarily to connect with nature every day. (We do spend 3 or 4 months somewhere warm in the winter so that way we have the best of both worlds!). Whether it's going on long hikes in the wilderness to remote lakes, horseback riding in the open pasture on my trusty equine companion, or soaking my body at a thermal hot spring, this place and its majestic beauty had me at *yeehaw.*

Well, technically it had me since my dad moved up here when I was a boy. As I have mentioned, I split my time growing up between the beaches of Sarasota, Florida, and the mountains of Red Lodge, Montana—a combination of cultures that formed me into what my friend Derek calls a "hippy cowboy."

After traveling around the world, I've come to realize that the ability to step into nature is missing for far too many people. One reason it is missing is that human beings have been destroying it. Deforestation, urbanization, and infrastructure development have destroyed natural habitats and fragmented the remaining areas. This can reduce biodiversity, decimate animal populations, and limit the availability of natural spaces for Happy Hustlin' Nature Connection.

If you find yourself living somewhere that you can't easily access a forest with some sort of hiking trails, a beach, a green space park, or even a big backyard, maybe you should consider making a move. You need nature; we *all* do! According to NatureQuant,[2] the science is indisputable: nature exposure provides profound mental and physical health improvements.

Through NatureQuant's innovative software, you can actually plug in your current home address and receive a Nature Score. Check out *The Happy Hustle™ Podcast* Episode #297 with Jared

Hanley, CEO of NatureQuant & Research Scientist to learn why increased nature exposure equals a healthier, longer life.

If you aren't getting outside and connecting regularly with nature, it's time to make a plan for change. I want you to have a Blissfully Balanced life, but for that to happen, you have to make

an honest assessment of whether or not you are in an ideal place to make that happen. And sometimes that honest assessment will lead you to a decision, a crossroads in which you must determine which path to take. Especially now with all the online remote work, it is easier than ever before to work yet still be surrounded by nature.

One of my favorite pics of me fly-fishing at Lake McDonald in Glacier National Park

I found myself at that crossroads while living in South Florida. Sure, I would regularly go kayaking, fishing, bike riding, and to the beach and state parks, but even still it wasn't enough for me. I knew I wanted more nature and fewer people.

My heart was in Montana, and my soul craved a self-sufficient sustainable ranch using regenerative practices, so that's exactly what I am building. What does your soul crave? How will you go forward from here and incorporate nature more into your and your family's life?

THE TRIP OF A LIFETIME: MONTANA MASTERMIND EPIC CAMPING ADVENTURE

Since we're talking about Nature Connection, I wanted to share again with you a way you can tap into your primal nature and disconnect to reconnect with your higher self.

Imagine a digital detox like no other. Hiking into nature's glory, over beautiful mountains and across rushing rivers, and camping out in the backcountry wilderness with a group of like-minded Happy Hustlers for 5 days.

We business mastermind (sharing wins, embracing losses, and collectively brainstorming for one another), crush primal workouts, take natural cold baths in alpine lakes, embark on deep meditations, learn primitive survival skills from experts, practice the art of fly-fishing, and much more... all while epic lifelong friendships and memories are forged.

This is the August 2022 Montana Mastermind crew of world-class Happy Hustlin' entrepreneurs soaking up nature's glory!

In addition, we eat nutritious and delicious healthy food prepared by a professional backcountry chef and get it all captured by a professional videographer and photographer for you to then leverage that content in your business later.

Fly-fishing with my trusty pup Ninja

We hang out around the campfire and tell stories and howl at the moon under the breathtaking stars of Big Sky Country Montana. This is truly one of my favorite times of the year. It allows me (and everyone who joins) to completely reset while tapping into nature and our primal selves on a whole new level—not to mention, mixing business with pleasure all the while!

If you would like to learn more and see if it is a fit for you, head over to thehappyhustle.com/hub and apply today. Spots are limited and life-changing fun is guaranteed. Yeehaw!

The July 2023 Montana Mastermind crew ready to embark on our epic adventure up the mountain!

🎯 ALIGNMENT TAKEAWAY

Ask yourself if your current environment provides the level of nature you desire. If not, seriously consider making a change. You know I love Montana, but just so everyone doesn't up and move here, let me also mention that there are a ton of grizzly bears (as my cousin Paul dramatically learned), and winter temps can drop to more than 50° *below* zero at times! So if that's not your personal cup of tea, find a place that suits your family's nature needs!

Or, if actually moving to a new location isn't in the cards for you, consider traveling to areas rich in nature. I love exploring other wild places that this beautiful Earth offers, and look for short-term rentals and enjoy extended stays. If you're a Happy Hustlin' digital nomad, this is a no-brainer.

If regular travel isn't an option right now, and you have to stay in an urban jungle, you can still Happy Hustle your Nature Connection. Visit local parks, gardens, and green spaces, which can provide a break from the "cages" of city life. Incorporate plants and greenery into your home or office environment to bring a bit of nature indoors. Take up urban gardening, or vertical farming, which can help to provide fresh produce while also creating a more sustainable and nature-filled urban environment. **Keep the Triple Bottom Line top of mind in your career.** Become an eco-warrior and conscious consumer, supporting sustainable companies! Focus on creating harmony between People, Planet, and Profits! Whatever you do, start to Happy Hustle more Nature Connection my friend!

DAILY ACTION TASKS TO HAPPY HUSTLE:

Nature Connection

1. Go for a 15-minute walk outside! Bonus points if you leave behind your phone and headphones!
2. Schedule a minimum 3-day camping trip for this month.
3. Research sustainable alternatives for your most common unsustainable purchases.

😀 EMBARRASSING FUN FACT

When I was in my early teens, I once was dared in the wilderness to swim naked across a freezing river in exchange for $20. I got about halfway back from this ice-cold swim and my whole body locked up from the snowy ice-chilled water. I had to be rescued with a rope, and to make matters worse, as I was nearly lifeless, nakedly crawling up the shore, a Girl Scout troop was hiking past us on the trail. Yep, great timing...

POWERFUL RESOURCES

Books:

Let My People Go Surfing by Yvon Chouinard
The Practice of Natural Movement: Reclaim Power, Health, and Freedom by Erwan Le Corre

Podcasts:

The Happy Hustle™ Podcast—Episode #297 with Jared Hanley, CEO of NatureQuant
No Barriers Podcast with Erik Weihenmayer

Movies:

Kiss The Ground
The Weight of Water

HAPPY HUSTLER SPOTLIGHT 💡

Yvon Chouinard

Yvon Chouinard is an American rock climber, environmentalist, and outdoor industry billionaire. His company, Patagonia, is known for its environmental focus while giving back to the land. He is for sure a Happy Hustler and can often be found surfing off the coast of California or climbing in the mountains of Wyoming.

He is a master tinkerer and created the outdoor behemoth Patagonia back in 1971 by initially selling rock climbers more advanced handmade gear.

He has done so many wonderful things for this planet it would be hard to list his true impact in this short spotlight. He is connected with nature more than any billionaire I know of and does more for the environment because of his visceral bond.

Yvon is an amazing entrepreneur who has not wavered in his mission, and his company gives back 1% of every dollar earned to causes that help to protect and serve Mother Earth.

He is an avid fly fisherman, climber, kayaker, adventurist, and indeed a Happy Hustler who knows how to balance nature, business, and the civilized world.

CHAPTER ELEVEN

BLISSFUL BALANCE

Life is like riding a bicycle. To keep your balance,
you must keep moving."

Albert Einstein

I t was 4:00 A.M. in Amsterdam. I woke up to 3 inches of water soaking my clothes and an overwhelming stench of sewage. Just an hour earlier, I had snuck into a crappy hostel room where my buddy was staying with 8 other people. I was broke—no money to even afford my own bed—so I had to sleep on the hard terrazzo floor underneath one of the bunk beds. Apparently, one of the dudes clogged the toilet and flooded the whole joint. Needless to say, my morale and self-worth were at an all-time low.

Wandering the Red Light District in Amsterdam, not my finest moment in time

On top of that, my eye was swollen from getting into a bar fight earlier in the Red Light District. I was sticking up for 2 girls who were being sexually harassed by 3 men on the dance floor during a pub crawl. Needless to say, I hope they learned their lesson, as they received far worse than a swollen eye.

Just a couple of weeks prior, I thought I had hit one of the lowest moments of my life after an all-night rager in Ibiza, the party island off the coast of Spain. I had fiesta'd at a foam party where they filled the club with foam from the floor to the ceiling—and lost all of my money, phone, wallet, shoes...and dignity.

I had been on an absolute bender. My body was run down. I was mentally spent. I was a hot mess. My sole focus at that time in my life was partying and women, not necessarily in that order. And now here I was, completely out of balance, sleeping on the floor and covered in sewer water with nowhere else to go.

Were you ever so out of balance that a rude awakening shook you to the core? Well, this was exactly that for me. I knew I needed to change my ways. I knew I needed to become a better version of myself and start prioritizing what was important. I was far from home and very lost.

When you're out of balance, life has a way of letting you know. Sometimes, it will show up in big, obvious ways, as swimming in sewage did for me. Other times, it may show up more slowly, in subtle ways, like a nagging feeling that something's not quite right with your life. Regardless of how life lets you know you're out of balance, the point is that you need to recognize it. When you know, you know.

And when that happens, the first step to making a change is admitting you're off the rails. I've done a lot of stupid stuff in my life. One nearly landed me in a casket. One actually did land me in jail for a brief stint! One led to me being held at gunpoint. Others landed me in the hospital. It took these lowest lows to get my attention and compel me to make a change and to then passionately pursue a better version of myself and my reality.

THE 10 ALIGNMENTS OF A HAPPY HUSTLER CAN BE A BLUEPRINT FOR BUILDING YOUR DREAM REALITY.

That day, in the pre-dawn hours in Amsterdam, I made a decision. I gave up my life of imbalance and hustlin' for a life of Blissful Balance and Happy Hustlin'.

I traded crime and fighting for operating with ultimate integrity and being the loving light. I traded partying and one-night stands for personal growth and monogamy. I traded in a faithless existence to a faithful journey with God.

I freely admit I was on a destructive path in my early years and am lucky I didn't end up in prison or worse. I know firsthand just how much sweeter life can be with the proper framework and mindset, both of which I hope you've learned in this book.

The 10 Alignments of a Happy Hustler can be a blueprint for building your dream reality. The framework you just learned is timeless. It truly is a way to systematically harmonize ambition and well-being. If implemented, it will genuinely provide you with the freedom and fulfillment—and most importantly, the balance and joy—that you desire.

BALANCE = HAPPINESS!

My friend, know that balance is not a final destination, but rather a never-ending journey. It is the not-so-secret secret to unlocking a life you truly love, one that legit leaves you overflowing with gratitude and emotion. It requires self-quantification, pivots, and adjustments along the way, but it is oh so worth it. For when you hit that homeostasis of Happy Hustlin', there's little that can compare.

Let me just say congratulations on making it this far. I am super stoked for you! The fact that you're reading this right now means that you are well on your way to being a Happy Hustler. Now it's time to finish strong!

To recap, the keys to creating and maintaining this Blissful Balance we've been talking about throughout this whole book are two things:

1. **Measure yourself in each of The 10 Alignments every Sunday evening (1-5) and use a Blissful Balancer fridge magnet every week to track your balance in real time... what you measure you can manage.**

2. **Give each Alignment (and its Action Task) equal importance, but *focus* on just one at a time. That means being fully immersed and present with the task at hand.**

Whether it's a Zoom meeting for your business (Impactful Work), a date night with your lover (Loving Relationships), or playing pick-up soccer with your buddies (Passionate Hobbies), each task is equally important to your Happy Hustle but should be focused on one at a time.

See, the problem is most people are thinking about their work when they are with their family and thinking about their family when they are at work, thereby doing neither effectively nor being fully present in either. *Don't let this be you any longer.* When you are doing something, go all out and be there, fully present and immersed.

Now, at times, your life will indeed become out of balance. You may be working on a particular project with a time-sensitive deadline or training for a big event, and most of your effort each day may revolve around achieving the task at hand. And that's ok. However, it is essential to get back to a beacon of balance—a place of harmony between your professional and personal life endeavors—after those focused sprints.

> **IT IS ESSENTIAL TO GET BACK TO A BEACON OF BALANCE—A PLACE OF HARMONY BETWEEN YOUR PROFESSIONAL AND PERSONAL LIFE ENDEAVORS— AFTER THOSE FOCUSED SPRINTS.**

Ultimately, balance is a moving target, an evolving, intangible goal. You can have it one day and then lose it the next. I find it helpful to think about balance with reference to the 4 seasons in nature.

THE 4 SEASONS

Seasons are marked not only by changing weather patterns, but by the stars, moons, and the sun. Native Americans knew the natural seasons and migrated their tribes accordingly. When the bears crawled into caves to hibernate, tribes knew winter was near. They believed that when the eagles flew close to the sun, spring was imminent. Native Americans were one with nature and respected the seasons.

Many of our selfish struggles and personal pains come from failing to recognize which season we are in. Swim upstream when you're intended to flow downstream in the season, and you'll be met with resistance and exhaustion.

In order to Happy Hustle a life full of Blissful Balance, determine what season you are in right now:

- **Winter**—a season of cold darkness where we reflect, regenerate, and rest.

- **Spring**—a season of nurturing and budding greatness, a time of incubation and preparation.

- **Summer**—a season to plant seeds, build, develop, hustle, and grow.

- **Fall**—a season where you reap the benefits of what you sowed in summer.

By clearly identifying which season you are in, you can then release any unnecessary stress or pressure you may place on yourself and plan life accordingly. If you are in summer and feel like you have been busting your butt without much return, you can rest assured that fall is just around the bend, and you will be rewarded for your hard work. Your seeds will grow, and you will harvest your crop. Don't rush the process or dare to cheat the laws of nature and life.

If you are in winter right now and feeling a bit more anxiety and even possibly depression, unsure of what your next moves should be, allow yourself to rest and feel the season. Don't fight it. Regenerate, and know that spring is near, the season when you will learn, incubate, and prepare to unleash your greatness within.

These life seasons can last days, weeks, or even months. And yes, sometimes a life season lasts more than a year. Some of your winters may be longer and harsher, while at other times, your life may feel like a never-ending summer.

If we understand and apply the lessons of each season of nature to our lives, those lessons will help us to achieve balance, peace, and happiness. Be deliberate with your actions in each season and know that the only true certainty in life is that change will happen. So, embrace the change, my friend, and live each season to its fullest!

> **Author's Note:** *It is a crying shame, an utter travesty, what many of our ancestors did (and still do) to Native Americans. Now I am not so naïve as to think there is anything I can do to right the wrongs or ease the pain suffered by these tribes and their people in the past. However, I am doing my damnedest to support and create a more unified present and future for them—and I hope you will, too. We can learn from the Native Americans while honoring their culture and wisdom.*

This is me with my Native American co-stars while shooting the documentary series Into the Wild Frontier *in Montana. They are kind, professional, and talented actors.*

◎ ALIGNMENT TAKEAWAY

There is and always will be "more to do." Cure yourself from the "more disease." Resist the pressure and accept the present peace. Create Zen for yourself by balancing your personal and professional life endeavors. **Remember Balance = Happiness.** But know that balance is ever teetering, like a see-saw. It requires constant tweaks, adjustments, and re-positioning in the form of honest introspection and daily inventory. I know it sounds daunting, but again, that is why I created the Blissful Balancer fridge magnet to easily quantify where you stand in your life in each of The 10 Alignments every single day.

Tools like this, parlayed with *The Journey: 10 Days to Become a Happy Hustler* online course, can be your best friend while breaking old, unbalanced habits. Remember, balance is a constant effort. Much like a tightrope walker, if you lose focus or stop moving forward while actively trying to stay balanced, you fall. And recognize what season you're currently in, be it winter, spring, summer, or fall. Then act suitably while giving yourself grace.

Be active in your pursuit of balance. Be balanced in your pursuit of happiness. And Happy Hustle a life you love!

☑ DAILY ACTION TASKS TO HAPPY HUSTLE:

Blissful Balance

1. Assess yourself in The 10 Alignments every Sunday evening, then prioritize change accordingly.

2. Recognize what season you are in and which is next.

3. Know that there is always more to do, so set parameters on your schedule to stop working at certain times.

😆 EMBARRASSING FUN FACT

I got 2 questionable tattoos while under the influence. One I got while in Bali. I sketched up a little smiley face with a red x over the eye and got it tatted on my ankle. It signifies that sometimes in life you get punched in the eye, but you can stay steady smilin' and persevere with positivity. Funny enough, this little smiley later became The Happy Hustle™ logo. Who woulda thought?!

The other tattoo was done on my wrist while under the influence of ayahuasca in the jungle of Costa Rica. It's a love light bulb with a spiritual ankh symbol in the middle that, once again, I drew up. Truthfully, it looks like a 10-year-old drew it. But the intent behind it is to signify a spiritual rebirth with the transition from the darkness into the light. I now strive to always shine bright with love and light.

🏋️🧠 POWERFUL RESOURCES

Books:
The 4-Hour Workweek by Tim Ferriss
The Monk Who Sold His Ferrari by Robin Sharma

Podcast:
Aubrey Marcus Podcast

Movie:
The Intern

Online Course:
The Journey: 10 Days to Become a Happy Hustler
(thehappyhustle.com/hub)

HAPPY HUSTLER SPOTLIGHT

Crystal & Mike Hill

This Happy Hustler Spotlight is a bit different. When I heard my friend Mike Hill's story about his late wife, Crystal, I knew I had to include it in the book. It truly can serve as a stark reminder of the sheer importance of Happy Hustlin' a blissfully balanced life. But rather than write it myself, I asked if Mike would share in his own words. So here it is, as follows:

> When my friend Cary asked me if I would share my wife's story, I was very conflicted. Her battle with balance was so challenging. Not just for her, but for our whole family. I frankly wasn't sure it was my story to tell, but ultimately realized it is a story that must be shared.

> When Crystal started a project, she was all in, dedicating 100% of herself to every task. But what happens when the force that compels us to do great things becomes a sense of identity that overtakes the rest of our life?

At the beginning of our marriage, Crystal would often commit our family's time, energy, and money to a community project. The entire family would participate, and we loved it. It brought us together and helped ingrain us into our community.

As time went on, the projects became larger, and they seemed to never end. The "fun" period of the projects started to fade for our family, but not for my love. She became a one-woman show, staying up all hours of the night, working for days on end. Eventually, she attracted a best friend to help, someone who was just as deeply passionate and dedicated as her. The two never backed away from a challenge, and they were inseparable.

Project after project would arise, and the dynamic duo would tackle them, slaying any obstacle placed in front of them. No matter how much time it took, no matter what. And I mean no matter what!

The first thing that had to go to achieve these fantastic feats was sleep. These projects had timelines! A couple of late nights turned into 3 or 4 hours max time spent in bed. Becoming a night owl was an easy way to escape any comments about finding balance.

However, "balance" isn't just a yoga phrase. The body needs it! Without balance, the body and mind will fight back.

Different areas of my wife's body and life started to shut down at different times. The energy she used to put into personal growth, self-care, and relationships all took a back seat to community projects.

The undercurrent of frustration that comes from a life out of balance became visible to nearly everyone who was really close to Crystal. Unfortunately, when allowed to continue for too long, these undercurrents of emotional energy take root in the body and start attacking the health.

Cancer arrived in 2018, and my love was dealt the blessing of Stage 0 breast cancer. I call it a blessing because this cancer was found early and easily removed with a simple surgery, requiring no chemo or ongoing treatments. It arrived to teach a lesson to us all.

Crystal found faith, stepped back from community service, got counseling, and started to practice some real self-care. Removing the drama that kept her body in fight or flight, engaging in mindfulness practices, and working on those areas of life that had been in decline became her focus.

But with a void in her creative side of life, Crystal found herself eventually craving opportunities to express her creative genius—anything to show the world just how talented and amazing she was.

Then an answer to her prayers arrived—her oldest daughter announced her engagement. There was a wedding to plan and create for! Long nights were spent on invitation designs, backdrops, wood cutting, painting... Crystal was back in her creative element.

The wedding was so beautiful that the venue owner asked her if she would host all of their weddings. For Crystal, this was a lifelong dream finally coming true. She threw herself into the work with all of the passion and purpose that she had formerly spent on the community projects.

After months of long days, no rest, no self-care, and no balance, my wife and I found ourselves sitting in front of her doctor. The doctor was brief. "You have non-defined liver cancer that has invaded your portal vein. There is nothing that can be done. You are not a candidate for transplant, so you have to get your affairs in order." Even though we didn't want to admit it, our time was up.

The cancer had gone unnoticed for over a year.

What if we had caught it earlier? What if she had received her regular MRIs? What if just a fraction of the energy she gave to the events had been put into her health and personal care? If any of these had happened, I believe my love would still be here today.

I write this today to share the importance of balance in life. Sadly, my wife—and our entire family—paid the ultimate price for living an unbalanced life out of alignment.

I hope Crystal's passing can serve as a cautionary tale of what can ensue when you are working too much and don't prioritize the other key elements of a balanced life. Please, take this simple concept of balance seriously and follow The 10 Alignments outlined in this book. While I can't guarantee they will save your life, I can say they will likely make it a heck of a lot more enjoyable.

—Mike Hill

CHAPTER TWELVE

_____

BRINGIN' IT ALL TOGETHER

I'd rather Happy Hustle 24/7 than slave 9 to 5.

Yours Truly

As this book is nearing its end, I want to impress upon you something imperative. None of the pages you just read covering Happy Hustlin', The 10 Alignments, and Blissful Balance will matter if you don't ACT upon the knowledge you've now acquired.

YOU MUST TAKE ACTION TO BECOME A HAPPY HUSTLER.

You must take action to become a Happy Hustler. You must adopt the mindset of a Happy Hustler and prioritize balance accordingly. As my close friend and *New York Times* best-selling author Rory Vaden says in his book, *Take the Stairs.*[1]

> *"It's not my right to tell you what you should do. I believe most of us already know what we should do. The problem is we don't do it. For most of us, it's not as much a matter of skill as it is a matter of will. Success means doing things you don't want to do. Action is the inevitable prerequisite for our success."*

Here's Rory and me cheesin' big. He is such an amazing human, helping mission-driven messengers from around the world become their best selves!

Man, does Rory nail it in that book! (It's a great read, by the way! Check it out.) But for real, you now have a choice to make. You can sit back and close this book after finishing these last couple of pages and go on with your life as it was.

You can go to work tomorrow potentially lacking purpose and do the necessary tasks to get by as you have in the past. You can show up as you have been, neither present nor living each moment to the fullest. You can allow valuable time with your family and friends to come and go. You can procrastinate a little longer with your health and fitness goals and continue living less than your optimized self.

You can put off doing your personal hobbies and having fun a bit longer. You can disregard Selfless Service and make helping others an afterthought that you get around to every now and then. You can continue to live unbalanced, not putting the Happy in your everyday Hustle.

But making those choices won't get you where you want to go! They won't help you create your dream reality. They won't earn you the Blissful Balance that results in real, everyday joy. Those decisions will ultimately lead you to an unfulfilling life of hustlin', but not happiness. And they may even lead you to burnout. On the other hand, there is another option...

You can take bold and decisive action! You can say *enough is enough*! You can adopt the Happy Hustler's mindset and go all in. You can create a life of Blissful Balance full of passion, purpose, and positive impact! You can systematically harmonize your ambition and well-being! You can hold yourself accountable with consequences. You can be diligent with how you spend your precious time, money, and energy.

You can also hold others around you accountable and raise their level as you do your own.

After all, we are all in this together. We can collectively make the world a happier place. Paraphrasing the late, great Zig Ziglar, *If you truly help others get what they want, you will ultimately get what you want!*

I am so grateful that you gave yourself the time to read this book. It has been my absolute honor to share with you The 10 Alignments of a Happy Hustler. To recap:

◦ Selfless Service

Remember **G.I.F.T.: G**ive **I**nsight, **F**inances, and **T**ime to individuals and causes that you feel called to help.

Happy Hustle Hack: *Schedule giving.*

◦ Optimized Health

Think **E.N.E.R.G.Y.:** Exercise, Nutrition, Environment, Rest, Gallon, and Youth. These are the pillars to optimizing your health. Exercise daily, eat healthy, clean up your home, prioritize deep sleep, drink a gallon of water a day, and utilize known anti-aging protocols to be your healthiest, optimized self!

Happy Hustle Hack: *What you don't eat is more important than what you do. Stop shoving crap down your piehole. Plus, stretch daily!*

◦ Unplug Digitally

Take a **B.R.E.A.K.: B**uild barriers, **R**echarge regularly, **E**liminate excess usage, **A**irplane mode approach, and **K**eep control and be disciplined. Use technology—don't let it use you!

Happy Hustle Hack: *30 minutes in the morning upon waking and 30 minutes before bed, be completely device free. And do a 24-hour digital detox on Sundays to recharge and start your week fresh and ready.*

Loving Relationships

Next time you experience conflict with your significant other, family member, friend, colleague, team member, etc., use the **L.O.V.E.R.** talk track to work through adversity: Listen, Observe, Voice, Empathize, & Repair.

Happy Hustle Hack: *If you want a 10, be 10. Plus, use a Love Calendar.*

Mindful Spirituality

Mindful spirituality cultivates inner strength, helps you appreciate life's blessings, and allows you to fully engage with the present moment, ultimately fostering a deeper sense of fulfillment and connection to your creator, yourself, and the world around you. Remind yourself daily to **C.I.T.S.** your ass down and just Chill In The Still.

Happy Hustle Hack: *Practice daily meditation, breathwork, and gratitude.*

Abundance Financially

Increase your financial literacy. Sharpen your sales sword by using the **R.O.A.D.M.A.P. $ales $trategy.** This can be your go-to itinerary for your future sales interactions. Rapport, Obstacle, Aspiration, Demonstration, Match, Ask, and Pull.

Happy Hustle Hack: *Create a system to spend, save, and invest your $$ wisely.*

○ **P**ersonal **D**evelopment

Use the **30-30-30 System for Guaranteed Growth**: 30 minutes reading in the morning, **30** minutes listening in the afternoon, **30** minutes watching in the evening—all inspirational and educational content. Grow and evolve every day.

Happy Hustle Hack: *Schedule your growth sessions.*

○ **P**assionate **H**obbies

Just have FUN doing things you enjoy regularly while prioritizing them with equal importance as work obligations. The **4 Factors of Fun**: 1) Does it bring me joy? 2) Will smiling & laughter ensue? 3) Do the others involved raise my vibration? 4) Will I grow?

Happy Hustle Hack: *Do FUN things you love to do a minimum of 2x per week.*

○ **I**mpactful **W**ork

Use the **HUSTLE-DOTE**. Do something that excites your soul, infuses your passion and your purpose, and makes a positive impact while creating income.

Happy Hustle Hack: *Figure out what problem you feel called to solve, who exactly you want to solve it for, and your uniqueness in solving it... then your Hustlin' Why behind it!*

₀ **Nature Connection**

Connect with nature every day in some way and enjoy and protect Mother Earth. Focus on the **Triple Bottom Line**, PPP: People, Planet, Profits.

Happy Hustle Hack: *Commit to a 15-minute daily walk outside. Protect our planet by voting with your dollar and supporting conscious, sustainable companies.*

That is what this book is all about. The 10 Alignments are your path to the Blissfully Balanced promised land. I'm telling ya, when I started implementing the 5 Stages to Happy Hustlin' in each alignment, and actually holding myself accountable in each, my life transformed and my happiness skyrocketed. *The same will happen for you.*

Remember, there is a systematic way to raise your score in each area of life.

The 5 Stages to Happy Hustlin' in Each Alignment:

1. Do an honest audit of your reality and feel gratitude for where you are.

2. Define your vision for success; what does a 5 look like in this Alignment?

3. Reverse engineer the process and create a winning game plan.

4. Take massive action and execute! Manage your time and priorities accordingly.

5. Employ persistent consistency. Enjoy the journey Happy Hustlin' a life of passion, purpose, and positive impact.

So wherever you are in each Alignment, you have a framework for improvement. When implementing all of this, the big thing is to push past the FEAR (False Evidence Appearing Real) that may be holding your transformation back.

Want to know how you get past the fear? With action.

Action is the cure for fear. And balance is the cure for avoiding burnout. Even if you're scared or don't feel like it, make the necessary changes. Take action!

I'm sure you're getting sick of me saying this by now, but maybe you need to hear it! I know I did. I needed that kick in the butt from my mentors and the books I read. And boy am I glad I got it.

Have the discipline to take what you've learned, implement it, and watch your life transform. Don't let fear hold you back any longer. Your time is now. The Happy Hustle™ is here to show you a better way to create balanced alignment both personally and professionally. It's here to help you systematically harmonize ambition and well-being, a way to find joy in the journey while in the pursuit of your goals and dream reality. A way to increase the freedom, fulfillment, and fun in your everyday life. Don't let this be the end, but rather just the beginning. Become the best Happy Hustler you can be.

To wrap up this book in style, I've got several action items for you. Links to every Happy Hustlin' resource I mentioned in this book can be found at thehappyhustle.com/hub. This hub was created

SCAN ME

especially for you reading this book, so you can navigate everywhere you need to go, not just once, but frequently from now on! I would bookmark it on your devices. It is regularly updated with the latest Happy Hustlin' info, insights, PDFs, links, tips, tools, and tactics to help you Happy Hustle your dream reality.

You can go to thehappyhustle.com/hub, or you can scan this QR code and dive right in!

Here's a checklist of action items to pursue if you want to Happy Hustle beyond the book:

1. **Take the Happy Hustler Assessment** every week and prioritize change accordingly. Again, this a crucial piece to the puzzle as what you measure you can manage.

2. Use a **Blissful Balancer fridge magnet** to measure and track your balance every day! Remember, this is a way to track your progress and balance in The 10 Alignments in real time. Plus it's intentionally analog so you don't need to be on your devices to keep track!

3. Next, join our awesome **Facebook group** "Happy Hustlers Worldwide" (yes, people still do FB groups). We are creating a movement, gamifying balance with The S.O.U.L.M.A.P.P.I.N.™ System, and this tribe's vibe is epic.

4. **Check out *The Journey: 10 Days to Become a Happy Hustler* online course.** This is some of my best work distilled into a power-packed step-by-step video course that helps you implement The 10 Alignments and everything you just read into your everyday life!

5. Listen to our top .5% globally ranked *The Happy Hustle™ Podcast* for educational, inspirational, and entertaining episodes with some of the world's greatest Happy Hustlers!

6. Send the **FREE PDF download of The Happy Hustle™ ebook** to a friend in need. Spread the good word and help create more happiness in this world.

7. If you're an online entrepreneur and feeling froggy, leap by applying to join **The Happy Hustle™ Club** to connect regularly with a tribe of Happy Hustlers who are crushing personal and professional goals! Get expert mentorship, gamified accountability, and an awesome community to help you Happy Hustle on your journey!

8. If you want to take it a step further, check out The Happy Hustle Masterminds! We host multiple events every year for high-performing entrepreneurs, from skiing/snowboarding trips, to biohacking health intensives, to couplepreneur workshops, to camping retreats. Each event is intentionally curated to instill The 10 Alignments while mixing business with pleasure! Especially if you enjoy the great outdoors, apply for the **Montana Mastermind Epic Camping Adventure** and see if it's a fit. Talk about one helluva good time digitally detoxing in the beautiful backcountry wilderness!

9. If you are the leader of a company and want to implement The Happy Hustle™ into your company culture to systematically enhance employee happiness and productivity, check out our Company Happiness Program.

10. Your ultimate call to action: get out there and Happy Hustle *your* dream reality!

Again, links to all 10 of the above calls to action can be found at thehappyhustle.com/hub! There is also Happy Hustler swag, in case you want to rep the movement. You know a good Happy Hustler couldn't miss out on merch like dope hats, tees, etc.!

I truly hope you enjoyed the lessons, spotlights, stories, ridiculously cheesy jokes, Happy Hustle Hacks, embarrassing fun facts, and everything in-between. I feel truly blessed in this beautiful thing called life. Sure, there has been plenty of adversity along the way, much of which I left out, as I felt it was not relevant to you at this time.

However, I do wish I had the foresight and knowledge that I now have. This is why I wanted to write this book and share the lessons learned. My hope is that maybe, just maybe, if you are on the brink of burnout, hustlin' but not happy, or living a life of imbalance, that you will now be armed with the information needed to transform your reality. Within these pages, you have the power to create a blissfully balanced life that you love. I've offered you a system to infuse more freedom, fulfillment, fun, and financial abundance, which if utilized could very well lead to a life beyond your wildest dreams.

My ultimate goal is for us all to systematically harmonize ambition and well-being. I want to prove that you do not have to settle for what life gives you. You can create the life that you desire. With hustle, a clear vision, and a willingness to persist, anything is achievable. By deciding what you want and what you are willing to do for it, you can begin the journey down the road of Happy Hustlin' to go get it while using The 10 Alignments to keep you Blissfully Balanced along the way.

YOU CAN CREATE THE LIFE THAT YOU DESIRE. WITH HUSTLE, A CLEAR VISION, AND A WILLINGNESS TO PERSIST, ANYTHING IS ACHIEVABLE.

Again, it has been a real honor writing for you. From the bottom, top, and middle of my heart, I want to thank you for your time. Thank you for sticking with me page by page, reading my outlandish stories, and putting up with my silly humor.

Thank you for being a part of my journey and learning how to Happy Hustle your own. I can hardly believe it is coming to an end. However, it's not goodbye; it's see ya later, as I know a couple more books are coming your way in the near future. Stand by, my friend.

To be honest, I now know what authors mean when they say writing is a "real labor of love." Holy guacamole has this damn thing taken love, energy, and focus on another level to finish it!

I can only hope and pray that my writing makes a positive impact on you in some way. This is an amazing adventure we are all on. Don't take a moment of it for granted. Life can change in an instant. So, love deeper, be kinder, and create blissful balance.

Manifest your dreams and never stop Happy Hustlin', my friend.

I love you and am so grateful for you.

Your friend and fellow Happy Hustler,

Cary Jack

Get in baby; it's time to Happy Hustle a life you love!

ACKNOWLEDGMENTS

To my beautiful wife Steph, for supporting The Happy Hustle™ since its inception, including the late-night writing benders and weekend cabin getaways. I love and cherish you and couldn't be more grateful to be doing life together. Especially blessed to be raising a son together. Kaizen and I are lucky to have you!

To my ma, for taking this thing to the finish line with years of editing and feedback. You rock. Love ya.

To my brother Grant, my business partner and best friend, for always being my ride or die. Here's to positively changing the world together.

To my sister Megan, for being unapologetically you and standing up for what you believe in. Thank you for making this a better book.

To my dad, for instilling wisdom and work ethic. Thanks for always being there.

To my cousin Jason, founder of Studio217, who did the original cover design, The Happy Hustle™ logo, swag, you name it—the guy has been my go-to for branding and is a rockstar. Thanks, primo.

To my amazing Happy Hustle team, especially Connie who helped support me throughout the entire book process, y'all are family.

To the incredible StoryBuilders team, you folks are true professionals. Major shout out to Bill, Jen, and Akemi, who helped make this Version 2.0 a far better book than I could have ever created alone.

To all of my family, friends, and Happy Hustle Club members who have supported The Happy Hustle™ in ways both big and small, you know who you are.

And to YOU, who this book is truly for. Allow this to help you put the Happy in your Hustle for life. I am so grateful for you reading this!

CHAPTER NOTES

Introduction

1. Gallup.com. 2023. "State of the Global Workplace: 2023 Report." Accessed June 19, 2023. https://www.gallup.com/workplace/349484/state-of-the-global-workplace.aspx.

2. "Essential Entrepreneur Burnout Statistics in 2024." ZipDo. Accessed April 8, 2024. https://zipdo.co/statistics/entrepreneur-burnout#:~:text=30%25%20of%20entrepreneurs%20admit%20they

3. Haden, Jeff. "A New Study Says 75 Percent of Entrepreneurs Are Concerned about Their Mental Health." inc.com, May 18, 2023. https://www.inc.com/jeff-haden/a-new-study-says-75-percent-of-entrepreneurs-are-concerned-about-their-mental-health.html

4. Bellet, Clement, De Neve, Jan-Emmanuel & Ward, George. 2019. "Does Employee Happiness Have an Impact on Productivity?" Saïd Business School WP 2019-13, Available at SSRN: https://ssrn.com/abstract=3470734 or http://dx.doi.org/10.2139/ssrn.3470734

Alignment 2

1. Watson NF, Badr MS, Belenky G, Bliwise DL, Buxton OM, Buysse D, Dinges DF, Gangwisch J, Grandner MA, Kushida C, Malhotra RK, Martin JL, Patel SR, Quan SF, Tasali E. "Recommended amount of sleep for a healthy adult: a joint consensus statement of the American Academy of Sleep Medicine and Sleep Research Society." J Clin Sleep Med 2015;11(6):591–592. Accessed June 19, 2023. https://aasm.org/resources/pdf/pressroom/adult-sleep-duration-consensus.pdf

2. Taylor, Kory & Jones, Elizabeth. 2022. "Adult Dehydration." National Library of Medicine. Accessed June 19, 2023. https://www.ncbi.nlm.nih.gov/books/NBK555956/

3. David Sinclair. n.d. "Diet and Key Principles for Longevity." Healthnews.com. Accessed June 19, 2023. https://healthnews.com/longevity/healthspan/david-sinclair-diet-and-key-principles-for-longevity/

4. Sinclair. "Diet and Key Principles for Longevity."

Alignment 3

1. Pall, Martin. 2018. "Wi-Fi is an important threat to human health." *Environmental Research. Science Direct.* Accessed 02/25/24. https://www.sciencedirect.com/science/article/pii/S0013935118300355

2. Carr, Tara. 2016. "Motivating by the Pain Pleasure Principle." Wisconsin. University of Wisconsin Green Bay.

Alignment 4

1. "How Much of Communication is Nonverbal?" *UT Permian Basin.* https://online.utpb.edu/about-us/articles/communication/how-much-of-communication-is-nonverbal/

Alignment 5

1. Dfarhud, Dariush, Malmir, Maryam & Khanahmadi, Mohammad. 2014. "Happiness & Health: The Biological Factors—Systematic Review Article." *National Institute of Health. Iran J Public Health.* Accessed June 19, 2023. https://www.ncbi.nlm.nih.gov/pmc/articles/PMC4449495/

2. Zaccaro, Andrea et al. 2018. "How Breath-Control Can Change Your Life: A Systematic Review on Psycho-Physiological Correlates of Slow Breathing." *National Library of Medicine at National Center for Biotechnology Information.* Accessed June 19, 2023. https://www.ncbi.nlm.nih.gov/pmc/articles/PMC6137615

Alignment 9

1. Gallup.com. 2023. "State of the Global Workplace: 2023 Report." Accessed June 19, 2023. https://www.gallup.com/workplace/349484/state-of-the-global-workplace.aspx
2. Gallup.com. 2023. "State of the Global Workplace: 2023 Report." Accessed June 19, 2023. https://www.gallup.com/workplace/349484/state-of-the-global-workplace.aspx
3. Kahneman, Daniel & Angus Deaton. 2010. "High income improves evaluation of life but not emotional well-being." *Center for Health and Well-being*. Princeton. Princeton University. Accessed 02/25/24. https://www.princeton.edu/~deaton/downloads/deaton_kahneman_high_income_improves_evaluation_August2010.pdf

Alignment 10

1. Klepeis, N., Nelson, W., Ott, W. et al. 2011. "The National Human Activity Pattern Survey (NHAPS): a resource for assessing exposure to environmental pollutants." J Expo Sci Environ Epidemiol 11, 231–252. Accessed 02/25/24. https://doi.org/10.1038/sj.jea.7500165
2. NatureQuant. Accessed 02/25/24. https://www.naturequant.com/

Bringin' It All Together

1. Vaden, Rory. 2012. "Take the Stairs: 7 Steps to Achieving True Success." TarcherPerigee.

Stop flipping pages, and start Happy Hustlin' your dream reality!